Shakespeare
Explained

Henry IV, Part 1

JOSEPH SOBRAN

mc **Marshall Cavendish**
Benchmark
New York

Series consultant: Richard Larkin

Marshall Cavendish
99 White Plains Road
Tarrytown, New York 10591
www.marshallcavendish.us

Library of Congress Cataloging-in-Publication Data

Sobran, Joseph.
Henry IV, part 1 / by Joseph Sobran.
p. cm. -- (Shakespeare explained)
"A literary analysis of the play Henry IV, part 1. Includes information on
the history and culture of Elizabethan England"--Provided by publisher.
Includes bibliographical references and index.
ISBN 978-0-7614-3419-1
1. Shakespeare, William, 1564-1616. King Henry IV. Part 1--Juvenile
literature. 2. Shakespeare, William, 1564-1616. King Henry IV. Part
1--Examinations--Study guides. I. Title.

PR2810.S63 2009
822.3'3--dc22
2008037510

Photo research by: Linda Sykes
John Haynes/Royal Shakespeare Company: front cover; Bart Parren/istockphoto: 1; Neven
Mendrila/Shutterstock: 3; Raciro/istockphoto: 4; Art Parts RF: 6, 8, 13, 24, 25; Nik Wheeler/Corbis:
11; Portraitgalerie, Schloss Ambras, Innsbruck, Austria/Erich Lessing/Art Resource, NY: 18; AA
World Travel Library/Alamy: 20; Hideo Kurihara/Alamy: 22; Corbis/Sygma: 27; Andrew Fox/
Corbis: 30; Mary Evans Picture Library/Everett Collection: 37; Private Collection/Bridgeman Art
Library: 43; Tristram Kenton/Lebrecht Music: 46; Reg Wilson/Royal Shakespeare Company: 53;
The Granger Collection: 65; Courtesy Hollywood's Attic: 81; T Charles Erickson: 92.

Editor: Deborah Grahame
Publisher: Michelle Bisson
Art Director: Anahid Hamparian
Series Design: Kay Petronio

Printed in Malaysia
1 3 5 6 4 2

Contents

Shakespeare and His World

WILLIAM SHAKESPEARE, OFTEN NICKNAMED "THE BARD," IS, BEYOND ANY COMPARISON, THE MOST TOWERING NAME IN ENGLISH LITERATURE. MANY CONSIDER HIS PLAYS THE GREATEST EVER WRITTEN. HE STANDS OUT EVEN AMONG GENIUSES.

Yet the Bard is also closer to our hearts than lesser writers, and his tremendous reputation should neither intimidate us nor prevent us from enjoying the simple delights he offers in such abundance. It is as if he had written for each of us personally. As he himself put it, "One touch of nature makes the whole world kin."

Such tragedies as *Hamlet*, *Romeo and Juliet*, and *Macbeth* are world-famous, still performed on stage and in films. These and others have also been adapted for radio, television, opera, ballet, pantomime, novels, comic books, and other media. Two of the best ways to become familiar with them are to watch some of the many fine movies that have been made of them and to listen to recordings of them by some of the world's great actors.

Even Shakespeare's individual characters have a life of their own, like real historical figures. Hamlet is still regarded as the most challenging role ever written for an actor. Roughly as many whole books have been written about Hamlet, an imaginary character, as about actual historical figures such as Abraham Lincoln and Napoleon Bonaparte.

Shakespeare created an amazing variety of vivid characters. One of Shakespeare's most peculiar traits was that he loved his characters so much—even some of his villains and secondary or comic characters—that at times he let them run away with the play, stealing attention from his heroes and heroines.

So in *A Midsummer Night's Dream* audiences remember the absurd and lovable fool Bottom the Weaver better than the lovers who are the main characters. Romeo's friend Mercutio is more fiery and witty than Romeo himself; legend claims that Shakespeare said he had to kill Mercutio or Mercutio would have killed the play.

Shakespeare also wrote dozens of comedies and historical plays, as well as nondramatic poems. Although his tragedies are now regarded as his greatest works, he freely mixed them with comedy and history. And his sonnets are among the supreme love poems in the English language.

It is Shakespeare's mastery of the English language that keeps his words familiar to us today. Every literate person knows dramatic lines such as "Wherefore art thou Romeo?"; "My kingdom for a horse!"; "To be or not to be: that is the question"; "Friends, Romans, countrymen, lend me your ears"; and "What fools these mortals be!" Shakespeare's sonnets are noted for their sweetness: "Shall I compare thee to a summer's day?"

PLAY OUT
THE PLAY

SHAKESPEARE'S LANGUAGE

WITHOUT A DOUBT, SHAKESPEARE WAS THE GREATEST MASTER OF THE ENGLISH LANGUAGE WHO EVER LIVED. BUT JUST WHAT DOES THAT MEAN?

Shakespeare's vocabulary was huge, full of references to the Bible as well as Greek and Roman mythology. Yet his most brilliant phrases often combine very simple and familiar words:

"WHAT'S IN A NAME? THAT WHICH WE CALL A ROSE BY ANY OTHER NAME WOULD SMELL AS SWEET."

He has delighted countless millions of readers. And we know him only through his language. He has shaped modern English far more than any other writer.

Or, to put it in more personal terms, you probably quote his words several times every day without realizing it, even if you have never suspected that Shakespeare could be a source of pleasure to you.

So why do so many English-speaking readers find his language so difficult? It is our language, too, but it has changed so much that it is no longer quite the same language—nor a completely different one, either.

Shakespeare's English and ours overlap without being identical. He would have some difficulty understanding us, too! Many of our everyday words and phrases would baffle him.

Shakespeare, for example, would not know what we meant by a *car,* a *radio,* a *movie,* a *television,* a *computer,* or a *sitcom,* since these things did not even exist in his time. Our old-fashioned term *railroad train* would be unimaginable to him, far in the distant future. We would have to explain to him (if we could) what *nuclear weapons, electricity,* and *democracy* are. He would also be a little puzzled by common expressions such as *high-tech, feel the heat, approval ratings, war criminal, judgmental,* and *whoopie cushion.*

So how can we call him "the greatest master of the English language"? It might seem as if he barely spoke English at all! (He would, however, recognize much of our dirty slang, even if he pronounced it slightly differently. His plays also contain many racial insults to Jews, Africans, Italians, Irish, and others. Today he would be called "insensitive.")

Many of the words of Shakespeare's time have become archaic. Words like *thou, thee, thy, thyself,* and *thine,* which were among the most common words in the language in Shakespeare's day, have all but disappeared today. We simply say *you* for both singular and plural, formal and familiar. Most other modern languages have kept their *thou.*

Sometimes the same words now have different meanings. We are apt to be misled by such simple, familiar words as *kind, wonderful, waste, just,* and *dear,* which he often uses in ways that differ from our usage.

Shakespeare also doesn't always use the words we expect to hear, the words that we ourselves would naturally use. When we might automatically say, "I beg your pardon" or just "Sorry," he might say, "I cry you mercy."

Often a glossary and footnotes will solve all three of these problems for us. But it is most important to bear in mind that Shakespeare was often hard for his first audiences to understand. Even in his own time his rich language was challenging. And this was deliberate. Shakespeare was inventing his own kind of English. It remains unique today.

A child doesn't learn to talk by using a dictionary. Children learn first by sheer immersion. We teach babies by pointing at things and saying their names. Yet the toddler always learns faster than we can teach! Even as babies we are geniuses. Dictionaries can help us later, when we already speak and read the language well (and learn more slowly).

So the best way to learn Shakespeare is not to depend on the footnotes and glossary too much, but instead to be like a baby: just get into the flow of the language. Go to performances of the plays or watch movies of them.

THE LANGUAGE HAS A MAGICAL WAY OF TEACHING ITSELF, IF WE LET IT. THERE IS NO REASON TO FEEL STUPID OR FRUSTRATED WHEN IT DOESN'T COME EASILY.

Hundreds of phrases have entered the English language from *Hamlet* alone, including "to hold, as t'were, the mirror up to nature"; "murder most foul"; "the thousand natural shocks that flesh is heir to"; "flaming youth"; "a countenance more in sorrow than in anger"; "the play's the thing"; "neither a borrower nor a lender be"; "in my mind's eye"; "something is rotten in the state of Denmark"; "alas, poor Yorick"; and "the lady doth protest too much, methinks."

From other plays we get the phrases "star-crossed lovers"; "what's in a name?"; "we have scotched the snake, not killed it"; "one fell swoop"; "it was Greek to me;" "I come to bury Caesar, not to praise him"; and "the most unkindest cut of all"—all these are among our household words. In fact, Shakespeare even gave us the expression "household words." No wonder his contemporaries marveled at his "fine filed phrase" and swooned at the "mellifluous and honey-tongued Shakespeare."

Shakespeare's words seem to combine music, magic, wisdom, and humor:

"THE COURSE OF TRUE LOVE NEVER DID RUN SMOOTH."

"HE JESTS AT SCARS THAT NEVER FELT A WOUND."

"THE FAULT, DEAR BRUTUS, IS NOT IN OUR STARS, BUT IN OURSELVES, THAT WE ARE UNDERLINGS."

"COWARDS DIE MANY TIMES BEFORE THEIR DEATHS; THE VALIANT NEVER TASTE OF DEATH BUT ONCE."

"NOT THAT I LOVED CAESAR LESS, BUT THAT I LOVED ROME MORE."

"THERE ARE MORE THINGS IN HEAVEN AND EARTH, HORATIO, THAN ARE DREAMT OF IN YOUR PHILOSOPHY."

"BREVITY IS THE SOUL OF WIT."

"THERE'S A DIVINITY THAT SHAPES OUR ENDS, ROUGH-HEW THEM HOW WE WILL."

Four centuries after Shakespeare lived, to speak English is to quote him. His huge vocabulary and linguistic fertility are still astonishing. He has had a powerful effect on all of us, whether we realize it or not. We may wonder how it is even possible for a single human being to say so many memorable things.

Only the King James translation of the Bible, perhaps, has had a more profound and pervasive influence on the English language than Shakespeare. And, of course, the Bible was written by many authors over many centuries, and the King James translation, published in 1611, was the combined effort of many scholars.

EARLY LIFE

So who, exactly, was Shakespeare? Mystery surrounds his life, largely because few records were kept during his time. Some people have even doubted his identity, arguing that the real author of Shakespeare's plays must have been a man of superior formal education and wide experience. In a sense such doubts are a natural and understandable reaction to his rare, almost miraculous powers of expression, but some people feel that the doubts themselves show a lack of respect for the supremely human poet.

Most scholars agree that Shakespeare was born in the town of Stratford-upon-Avon in the county of Warwickshire, England, in April 1564. He was baptized, according to local church records, Gulielmus (William) Shakspere (the name was spelled in several different ways) on April 26 of that year. He was one of several children, most of whom died young.

His father, John Shakespeare (or Shakspere), was a glove maker and, at times, a town official. He was often in debt or being fined for unknown delinquencies, perhaps failure to attend church regularly. It is suspected that John was a "recusant" (secret and illegal) Catholic, but there is no proof. Many

SHAKESPEARE'S CHILDHOOD HOME IS CARED FOR BY AN INDEPENDENT CHARITY, THE SHAKESPEARE BIRTHPLACE TRUST, IN STRATFORD-UPON-AVON, WARWICKSHIRE, ENGLAND.

scholars have found Catholic tendencies in Shakespeare's plays, but whether Shakespeare was Catholic or not we can only guess.

At the time of Shakespeare's birth, England was torn by religious controversy and persecution. The country had left the Roman Catholic Church during the reign of King Henry VIII, who had died in 1547. Two of Henry's children, Edward and Mary, ruled after his death. When his daughter Elizabeth I became queen in 1558, she upheld his claim that the monarch of England was also head of the English Church.

Did William attend the local grammar school? He was probably entitled to, given his father's prominence in Stratford, but again, we face a frustrating absence of proof, and many people of the time learned to read very well without schooling. If he went to the town school, he would also have learned the rudiments of Latin.

We know very little about the first half of William's life. In 1582, when he was eighteen, he married Anne Hathaway, eight years his senior. Their first daughter, Susanna, was born six months later. The following year they had twins, Hamnet and Judith.

At this point William disappears from the records again. By the early 1590s we find "William Shakespeare" in London, a member of the city's leading acting company, called the Lord Chamberlain's Men. Many of Shakespeare's greatest roles, we are told, were first performed by the company's star, Richard Burbage.

Curiously, the first work published under (and identified with) Shakespeare's name was not a play but a long erotic poem, *Venus and Adonis*, in 1593. It was dedicated to the young Earl of Southampton, Henry Wriothesley.

Venus and Adonis was a spectacular success, and Shakespeare was immediately hailed as a major poet. In 1594 he dedicated a longer, more serious poem to Southampton, *The Rape of Lucrece*. It was another hit, and for many years, these two poems were considered Shakespeare's greatest works, despite the popularity of his plays.

" A PLAGUE OF ALL COWARDS, I SAY. "

SHAKESPEARE'S LANGUAGE

TODAY MOVIES, NOT LIVE PLAYS, ARE THE MORE POPULAR ART FORM. FORTUNATELY MOST OF SHAKESPEARE'S PLAYS HAVE BEEN FILMED, AND THE BEST OF THESE MOVIES OFFER AN EXCELLENT WAY TO MAKE THE BARD'S ACQUAINTANCE. RECENTLY, KENNETH BRANAGH HAS BECOME A RESPECTED CONVERTER OF SHAKESPEARE'S PLAYS INTO FILM.

Hamlet

Hamlet, Shakespeare's most famous play, has been well filmed several times. In 1948 Laurence Olivier won three Academy Awards—for best picture, best actor, and best director—for his version of the play. The film allowed him to show some of the magnetism that made him famous on the stage. Nobody spoke Shakespeare's lines more thrillingly.

The young Derek Jacobi played Hamlet in a 1980 BBC production of the play, with Patrick Stewart (now best known for *Star Trek, the Next Generation*) as the guilty king. Jacobi, like Olivier, has a gift for speaking the lines freshly; he never seems to be merely reciting the famous and familiar words. But whereas Olivier has animal passion, Jacobi is more intellectual. It is fascinating to compare the ways these two outstanding actors play Shakespeare's most complex character.

Franco Zeffirelli's 1990 *Hamlet*, starring Mel Gibson, is fascinating in a different way. Gibson, of course, is best known as an action hero, and he is not well suited to this supremely witty and introspective role, but Zeffirelli cuts the text drastically, and the result turns *Hamlet* into something that few people would have expected: a short, swift-moving action movie. Several of the other characters are brilliantly played.

Henry IV, Part One

The 1979 BBC Shakespeare series production does a commendable job in this straightforward approach to the play. Battle scenes are effective despite obvious restrictions in an indoor studio setting. Anthony Quayle gives jovial Falstaff a darker edge, and Tim Pigott-Smith's Hotspur is buoyed by some humor. Jon Finch plays King Henry IV with noble authority, and David Gwillim gives Hal a surprisingly successful transformation from boy prince to heir apparent.

Julius Caesar

No really good movie of *Julius Caesar* exists, but the 1953 film, with Marlon Brando as Mark Antony, will do. James Mason is a thoughtful Brutus, and John Gielgud, then ranked with Laurence Olivier among the greatest Shakespearean actors, plays the villainous Cassius. The film is rather dull, and Brando is out of place in a Roman toga, but it is still worth viewing.

Macbeth

Roman Polanski is best known as a director of thrillers and horror films, so it may seem natural that he should have done his 1971 *The Tragedy of Macbeth* as an often-gruesome slasher flick. But this is also one of the most vigorous of all Shakespeare films. Macbeth and his wife are played by Jon Finch and Francesca Annis, neither known for playing Shakespeare, but they are young and attractive in roles that are usually given to older actors, which gives the story a fresh flavor.

The Merchant of Venice

Once again the matchless Sir Laurence Olivier delivers a great performance as Shylock with his wife Joan Plowright as Portia in the 1974 TV film, adapted from the 1970 National Theater (of Britain) production. A 1980 BBC offering features Warren Mitchell as Shylock and Gemma Jones as Portia, with John Rhys-Davies as Salerio. The most recent production, starring Al Pacino as Shylock, Jeremy Irons as Antonio, and Joseph Fiennes as Bassanio, was filmed in Venice and released in 2004.

A Midsummer Night's Dream

Because of the prestige of his tragedies, we tend to forget how many comedies Shakespeare wrote—nearly twice the number of tragedies. Of these perhaps the most popular has always been the enchanting, atmospheric, and very silly masterpiece *A Midsummer Night's Dream*.

In more recent times several films have been made of *A Midsummer Night's Dream*. Among the more notable have been Max Reinhardt's 1935 black-and-white version, with Mickey Rooney (then a child star) as Puck.

Of the several film versions, the one starring Kevin Kline as Bottom and Stanley Tucci as Puck, made in 1999 with nineteenth-century costumes and directed by Michael Hoffman, ranks among the finest, and is surely one of the most sumptuous to watch.

Othello

Orson Welles did a budget European version in 1952, now available as a restored DVD. Laurence Olivier's 1965 film performance is predictably remarkable, though it has been said that he would only approach the part by honoring, even emulating, Paul Robeson's definitive interpretation that ran on Broadway in 1943. (Robeson was the first black actor to play Othello, the Moor of Venice, and he did so to critical acclaim, though sadly his performance was never filmed.) Maggie Smith plays a formidable Desdemona opposite Olivier, and her youth and energy will surprise younger audiences who know her only from the Harry Potter films. Laurence Fishburne brilliantly portrayed Othello in the 1995 film, costarring with Kenneth Branagh as a surprisingly human Iago, though Irène Jacob's Desdemona was disappointingly weak.

Romeo and Juliet

This, the world's most famous love story, has been filmed many times, twice very successfully over the last generation. Franco Zeffirelli directed a hit version in 1968 with Leonard Whiting and the rapturously pretty Olivia Hussey, set in Renaissance Italy. Baz Luhrmann made a much more contemporary version, with a loud rock score, starring Leonardo Di Caprio and Claire Danes, in 1996.

It seems safe to say that Shakespeare would have preferred Zeffirelli's movie, with its superior acting and rich, romantic, sun-drenched Italian scenery.

The Tempest

A 1960 Hallmark Hall of Fame production featured Maurice Evans as Prospero, Lee Remick as Miranda, Roddy McDowall as Ariel, and Richard Burton as Caliban. The special effects are primitive and the costumes are ludicrous, but it moves along at a fast pace. Another TV version aired in 1998 and was nominated for a Golden Globe. Peter Fonda played Gideon Prosper, and Katherine Heigl played his daughter Miranda Prosper. Sci-fi fans may already know that the classic 1956 film *Forbidden Planet* is modeled on themes and characters from the play.

Twelfth Night

Trevor Nunn adapted the play for the 1996 film he also directed in a rapturous Edwardian setting, with big names like Helena Bonham Carter, Richard E. Grant, Imogen Stubbs, and Ben Kingsley as Feste. A 2003 film set in modern Britain provides an interesting multicultural experience; it features an Anglo-Indian cast with Parminder Nagra (*Bend It Like Beckham*) playing Viola. For the truly intrepid, a twelve-minute silent film made in 1910 does a fine job of capturing the play through visual gags and over-the-top gesturing.

THESE FILMS HAVE BEEN SELECTED FOR SEVERAL QUALITIES: APPEAL AND ACCESSIBILITY TO MODERN AUDIENCES, EXCELLENCE IN ACTING, PACING, VISUAL BEAUTY, AND, OF COURSE, FIDELITY TO SHAKESPEARE. THEY ARE THE MOTION PICTURES WE JUDGE MOST LIKELY TO HELP STUDENTS UNDERSTAND THE SOURCE OF THE BARD'S LASTING POWER.

SHAKESPEARE'S THEATER

Today we sometimes speak of "live entertainment." In Shakespeare's day, of course, all entertainment was live, because recordings, films, television, and radio did not yet exist. Even printed books were a novelty.

In fact, most communication in those days was difficult. Transportation was not only difficult but slow, chiefly by horse and boat. Most people were illiterate peasants who lived on farms that they seldom left; cities grew up along waterways and were subject to frequent plagues that could wipe out much of the population within weeks.

Money—in coin form, not paper—was scarce and hardly existed outside the cities. By today's standards, even the rich were poor. Life was precarious. Most children died young, and famine or disease might kill anyone at any time. Everyone was familiar with death. Starvation was not rare or remote, as it is to most of us today. Medical care was poor and might kill as many people as it healed.

This was the grim background of Shakespeare's theater during the reign of Queen Elizabeth I, who ruled from 1558 until her death in 1603. During that period England was also torn by religious conflict, often violent, among Roman Catholics who were

ELIZABETH I, A GREAT PATRON OF POETRY AND THE THEATER, WROTE SONNETS AND TRANSLATED CLASSIC WORKS.

loyal to the Pope, adherents of the Church of England who were loyal to the queen, and the Puritans who would take over the country in the revolution of 1642.

Under these conditions, most forms of entertainment were luxuries that were out of most people's reach. The only way to hear music was to be in the actual physical presence of singers or musicians with their instruments, which were primitive by our standards.

One brutal form of entertainment, popular in London, was bear-baiting. A bear was blinded and chained to a stake, where fierce dogs called mastiffs were turned loose to tear him apart. The theaters had to compete with the bear gardens, as they were called, for spectators.

The Puritans, or radical Protestants, objected to bear-baiting and tried to ban it. Despite their modern reputation, the Puritans were anything but conservative. Conservative people, attached to old customs, hated them. They seemed to upset everything. (Many of America's first settlers, such as the Pilgrims who came over on the *Mayflower*, were dissidents who were fleeing the Church of England.)

Plays were extremely popular, but they were primitive, too. They had to be performed outdoors in the afternoon because of the lack of indoor lighting. Often the "theater" was only an enclosed courtyard. Probably the versions of Shakespeare's plays that we know today were not used in full, but shortened to about two hours for actual performance.

But eventually more regular theaters were built, featuring a raised stage extending into the audience. Poorer spectators (illiterate "groundlings") stood on the ground around it, at times exposed to rain and snow. Wealthier people sat in raised tiers above. Aside from some costumes, there were few props or special effects and almost no scenery. Much had to be imagined: Whole battles might be represented by a few actors with swords. Thunder might be simulated by rattling a sheet of tin offstage.

The plays were far from realistic and, under the conditions of the time, could hardly try to be. Above the rear of the main stage was a small balcony. (It was this balcony from which Juliet spoke to Romeo.) Ghosts and witches might appear by entering through a trapdoor in the stage floor.

Unlike the modern theater, Shakespeare's Globe Theater—he describes it as "this wooden O"—had no curtain separating the stage from the audience. This allowed intimacy between the players and the spectators.

THE RECONSTRUCTED GLOBE THEATER WAS COMPLETED IN 1997 AND IS LOCATED IN LONDON, JUST 200 YARDS (183 METERS) FROM THE SITE OF THE ORIGINAL.

The spectators probably reacted rowdily to the play, not listening in reverent silence. After all, they had come to have fun! And few of them were scholars. Again, a play had to amuse people who could not read.

The lines of plays were written and spoken in prose or, more often, in a form of verse called iambic pentameter (ten syllables with five stresses per line). There was no attempt at modern realism. Only males were allowed on the stage, so some of the greatest women's roles ever written had to be played by boys or men. (The same is true, by the way, of the ancient Greek theater.)

Actors had to be versatile, skilled not only in acting, but also in fencing, singing, dancing, and acrobatics. Within its limitations, the theater offered a considerable variety of spectacles.

Plays were big business, not yet regarded as high art, sponsored by important and powerful people (the queen loved them as much as the groundlings did). The London acting companies also toured and performed in the provinces. When plagues struck London, the government might order the theaters to be closed to prevent the spread of disease among crowds. (They remained empty for nearly two years from 1593 to 1594.)

As the theater became more popular, the Puritans grew as hostile to it as they were to bear-baiting. Plays, like books, were censored by the government, and the Puritans fought to increase restrictions, eventually banning any mention of God and other sacred topics on the stage.

In 1642 the Puritans shut down all the theaters in London, and in 1644 they had the Globe demolished. The theaters remained closed until Charles's son King Charles II was restored to the throne in 1660 and the hated Puritans were finally vanquished.

But, by then, the tradition of Shakespeare's theater had been fatally interrupted. His plays remained popular, but they were often rewritten by inferior dramatists and it was many years before they were performed (again) as he had originally written them.

THE ROYAL SHAKESPEARE THEATER, IN STRATFORD-UPON-AVON, WAS CLOSED IN 2007. A NEWLY DESIGNED INTERIOR WITH A 1000-SEAT AUDITORIUM WILL BE COMPLETED IN 2010.

Today, of course, the plays are performed both in theaters and in films, sometimes in costumes of the period (ancient Rome for *Julius Caesar*, medieval England for *Henry V*), sometimes in modern dress (*Richard III* has recently been reset in England in the 1930s).

PLAYS

In the England of Queen Elizabeth I, plays were enjoyed by all classes of people, but they were not yet respected as a serious form of art.

Shakespeare's plays began to appear in print in individual, or "quarto," editions in 1594, but none of these bore his name until 1598. Although his tragedies are now ranked as his supreme achievements, his name was first associated with comedies and with plays about English history.

The dates of Shakespeare's plays are notoriously hard to determine. Few performances of them were documented; some were not printed until decades after they first appeared on the stage. Mainstream scholars generally place most of the comedies and histories in the 1590s, admitting that this time frame is no more than a widely accepted estimate.

The three parts of *King Henry VI*, culminating in a fourth part, *Richard III*, deal with the long and complex dynastic struggle or civil wars known as the Wars of the Roses (1455–1487), one of England's most turbulent periods. Today it is not easy to follow the plots of these plays.

It may seem strange to us that a young playwright should have written such demanding works early in his career, but they were evidently very popular with the Elizabethan public. Of the four, only *Richard III*, with its wonderfully villainous starring role, is still often performed.

Even today, one of Shakespeare's early comedies, *The Taming of the Shrew*, remains a crowd-pleaser. (It has enjoyed success in a 1999 film adaptation, *10 Things I Hate About You*, with Heath Ledger and Julia Stiles.)

THE "REAL" SHAKESPEARE

AROUND 1850 DOUBTS STARTED TO SURFACE ABOUT WHO HAD ACTUALLY WRITTEN SHAKESPEARE'S PLAYS, CHIEFLY BECAUSE MANY OTHER AUTHORS, SUCH AS MARK TWAIN, THOUGHT THE PLAYS' AUTHOR WAS TOO WELL EDUCATED AND KNOWLEDGEABLE TO HAVE BEEN THE MODESTLY SCHOOLED MAN FROM STRATFORD.

Who, then, was the real author? Many answers have been given, but the three leading candidates are Francis Bacon, Christopher Marlowe, and Edward de Vere, Earl of Oxford.

Francis Bacon (1561–1626)

Bacon was a distinguished lawyer, scientist, philosopher, and essayist. Many considered him one of the great geniuses of his time, capable of any literary achievement, though he wrote little poetry and, as far as we know, no dramas. When people began to suspect that "Shakespeare" was only a pen name, he seemed like a natural candidate. But his writing style was vastly different from the style of the plays.

Christopher Marlowe (1564-1593)

Marlowe wrote several excellent tragedies in a style much like that of the Shakespeare tragedies, though without the comic blend. But he was reportedly killed in a mysterious incident in 1593, before most of the Bard's plays existed. Could his death have been faked? Is it possible that he lived on for decades in hiding, writing under a pen name? This is what his advocates contend.

Edward de Vere, Earl of Oxford (1550-1604)

Oxford is now the most popular and plausible alternative to the lad from Stratford. He had a high reputation as a poet and playwright in his day, but his life was full of scandal. That controversial life seems to match what the poet says about himself in the sonnets, as well as many events in the plays (especially *Hamlet*). However, he died in 1604, and most scholars believe this rules him out as the author of plays that were published after that date.

THE GREAT MAJORITY OF EXPERTS REJECT THESE AND ALL OTHER ALTERNATIVE CANDIDATES, STICKING WITH THE TRADITIONAL VIEW, AFFIRMED IN THE 1623 FIRST FOLIO OF THE PLAYS, THAT THE AUTHOR WAS THE MAN FROM STRATFORD. THAT REMAINS THE SAFEST POSITION TO TAKE, UNLESS STARTLING NEW EVIDENCE TURNS UP, WHICH, AT THIS LATE DATE, SEEMS HIGHLY UNLIKELY.

The story is simple: The enterprising Petruchio resolves to marry a rich young woman, Katherina Minola, for her wealth, despite her reputation for having a bad temper. Nothing she does can discourage this dauntless suitor, and the play ends with Kate becoming a submissive wife. It is all the funnier for being unbelievable.

With *Romeo and Juliet* the Bard created his first enduring triumph. This tragedy of "star-crossed lovers" from feuding families is known around the world. Even people with only the vaguest knowledge of Shakespeare are often aware of this universally beloved story. It has inspired countless similar stories and adaptations, such as the hit musical *West Side Story*.

By the mid-1590s Shakespeare was successful and prosperous, a partner in the Lord Chamberlain's Men. He was rich enough to buy New Place, one of the largest houses in his hometown of Stratford.

Yet, at the peak of his good fortune, came the worst sorrow of his life: Hamnet, his only son, died in August 1596 at the age of eleven, leaving nobody to carry on his family name, which was to die out with his two daughters.

Our only evidence of his son's death is a single line in the parish burial register. As far as we know, this crushing loss left no mark on Shakespeare's work. As far as his creative life shows, it was as if nothing had happened. His silence about his grief may be the greatest puzzle of his mysterious life, although, as we shall see, others remain.

During this period, according to traditional dating (even if it must be somewhat hypothetical), came the torrent of Shakespeare's mightiest works. Among these was another quartet of English history plays, this one centering on the legendary King Henry IV, including *Richard II* and the two parts of *Henry IV*.

Then came a series of wonderful romantic comedies: *Much Ado About Nothing*, *As You Like It*, and *Twelfth Night*.

ACTOR JOSEPH FIENNES PORTRAYED THE BARD IN THE 1998 FILM *SHAKESPEARE IN LOVE*, DIRECTED BY JOHN MADDEN.

In 1598 the clergyman Francis Meres, as part of a larger work, hailed Shakespeare as the English Ovid, supreme in love poetry as well as drama. "The Muses would speak with Shakespeare's fine filed phrase," Meres wrote, "if they would speak English." He added praise of Shakespeare's "sugared sonnets among his private friends." It is tantalizing; Meres seems to know something of the poet's personal life, but he gives us no hard information. No wonder biographers are frustrated.

Next the Bard returned gloriously to tragedy with *Julius Caesar*. In the play Caesar has returned to Rome in great popularity after his military triumphs.

Brutus and several other leading senators, suspecting that Caesar means to make himself king, plot to assassinate him. Midway through the play, after the assassination, comes one of Shakespeare's most famous scenes. Brutus speaks at Caesar's funeral. But then Caesar's friend Mark Antony delivers a powerful attack on the conspirators, inciting the mob to fury. Brutus and the others, forced to flee Rome, die in the ensuing civil war. In the end the spirit of Caesar wins after all. If Shakespeare had written nothing after *Julius Caesar*, he would still have been remembered as one of the greatest playwrights of all time. But his supreme works were still to come.

Only Shakespeare could have surpassed *Julius Caesar*, and he did so with *Hamlet* (usually dated about 1600). King Hamlet of Denmark has died, apparently bitten by a poisonous snake. Claudius, his brother, has married the dead king's widow, Gertrude, and become the new king, to the disgust and horror of Prince Hamlet. The ghost of old Hamlet appears to young Hamlet, reveals that he was actually poisoned by Claudius, and demands revenge. Hamlet accepts this as his duty, but cannot bring himself to kill his hated uncle. What follows is Shakespeare's most brilliant and controversial plot.

The story of *Hamlet* is set against the religious controversies of the Bard's time. Is the ghost in hell or purgatory? Is Hamlet Catholic or Protestant? Can revenge ever be justified? We are never really given the answers to such questions. But the play reverberates with them.

THE KING'S MEN

In 1603 Queen Elizabeth I died, and King James VI of Scotland became King James I of England. He also became the patron of Shakespeare's acting company, so the Lord Chamberlain's Men became the King's Men. From this point on, we know less of Shakespeare's life in London than in Stratford, where he kept acquiring property.

In the later years of the sixteenth century Shakespeare had been a rather elusive figure in London, delinquent in paying taxes. From 1602 to 1604 he lived, according to his own later testimony, with a French immigrant family named Mountjoy. After 1604 there is no record of any London residence for Shakespeare, nor do we have any reliable recollection of him or his whereabouts by others. As always, the documents leave much to be desired.

Nearly as great as *Hamlet* is *Othello*, and many regard *King Lear*, the heart-breaking tragedy about an old king and his three daughters, as Shakespeare's supreme tragedy. Shakespeare's shortest tragedy, *Macbeth*, tells the story of a Scottish lord and his wife who plot to murder the king of Scotland to gain the throne for themselves. *Antony and Cleopatra*, a sequel to *Julius Caesar*, depicts the aging Mark Antony in love with the enchanting queen of Egypt. *Coriolanus*, another Roman tragedy, is the poet's least popular masterpiece.

SONNETS AND THE END

The year 1609 saw the publication of Shakespeare's Sonnets. Of these 154 puzzling love poems, the first 126 are addressed to a handsome young man, unnamed, but widely believed to be the Earl of Southampton; the rest concern a dark woman, also unidentified. These mysteries are still debated by scholars.

Near the end of his career Shakespeare turned to comedy again, but it was a comedy of a new and more serious kind. Magic plays a large role in these late plays. For example, in *The Tempest*, the exiled duke of Milan, Prospero, uses magic to defeat his enemies and bring about a final reconciliation.

According to the most commonly accepted view, Shakespeare, not yet fifty, retired to Stratford around 1610. He died prosperous in 1616, and left a will that divided his goods, with a famous provision leaving his wife "my second-best bed." He was buried in the chancel of the parish church, under a tombstone bearing a crude rhyme:

> GOOD FRIEND, FOR JESUS SAKE FORBEARE
> TO DIG THE DUST ENCLOSED HERE.
> BLEST BE THE MAN THAT SPARES THESE STONES,
> AND CURSED BE HE THAT MOVES MY BONES.

This epitaph is another hotly debated mystery: Did the great poet actually compose these lines himself?

SHAKESPEARE'S GRAVE IN HOLY TRINITY CHURCH, STRATFORD-UPON-AVON. HIS WIFE, ANNE HATHAWAY, IS BURIED BESIDE HIM.

THE FOLIO

In 1623 Shakespeare's colleagues of the King's Men produced a large volume of the plays (excluding the sonnets and other poems) titled *The Comedies, Histories, and Tragedies of Mr. William Shakespeare* with a woodcut portrait—the only known portrait—of the Bard. As a literary monument it is priceless, containing our only texts of half the plays; as a source of biographical information it is severely disappointing, giving not even the dates of Shakespeare's birth and death.

Ben Jonson, then England's poet laureate, supplied a long prefatory poem saluting Shakespeare as the equal of the great classical Greek tragedians Aeschylus, Sophocles, and Euripides, adding that "He was not of an age, but for all time."

Some would later denigrate Shakespeare. His reputation took more than a century to conquer Europe, where many regarded him as semi-barbarous. His works were not translated before 1740. Jonson himself, despite his personal affection, would deprecate "idolatry" of the Bard. For a time Jonson himself was considered more "correct" than Shakespeare, and possibly the superior artist.

But Jonson's generous verdict is now the whole world's. Shakespeare was not merely of his own age, "but for all time."

"I COULD HAVE BETTER SPARED A BETTER MAN."

allegory—a story in which characters and events stand for general moral truths. Shakespeare never uses this form simply, but his plays are full of allegorical elements.

alliteration—repetition of one or more initial sounds, especially consonants, as in the saying "through thick and thin," or in Julius Caesar's statement, "veni, vidi, vici."

allusion—a reference, especially when the subject referred to is not actually named, but is unmistakably hinted at.

aside—a short speech in which a character speaks to the audience, unheard by other characters on the stage.

comedy—a story written to amuse, using devices such as witty dialogue (high comedy) or silly physical movement (low comedy). Most of Shakespeare's comedies were romantic comedies, incorporating lovers who endure separations, misunderstandings, and other obstacles but who are finally united in a happy resolution.

deus ex machina—an unexpected, artificial resolution to a play's convoluted plot. Literally, "god out of a machine."

dialogue—speech that takes place among two or more characters.

diction—choice of words for tone. A speech's diction may be dignified (as when a king formally addresses his court), comic (as when the ignorant grave diggers debate whether Ophelia deserves a religious funeral), vulgar, romantic, or whatever the dramatic occasion requires. Shakespeare was a master of diction.

Elizabethan—having to do with the reign of Queen Elizabeth I, from 1558 until her death in 1603. This is considered the most famous period in the history of England, chiefly because of Shakespeare and other noted authors (among them Sir Philip Sidney, Edmund Spenser, and Christopher Marlowe). It was also an era of military glory, especially the defeat of the huge Spanish Armada in 1588.

Globe—the Globe Theater housed Shakespeare's acting company, the Lord Chamberlain's Men (later known as the King's Men). Built in 1598, it caught fire and burned down during a performance of *Henry VIII* in 1613.

hyperbole—an excessively elaborate exaggeration used to create special emphasis or a comic effect, as in Montague's remark that his son Romeo's sighs are "adding to clouds more clouds" in *Romeo and Juliet*.

irony—a discrepancy between what a character says and what he or she truly believes, what is expected to happen and what really happens, or between what a character says and what others understand.

metaphor—a figure of speech in which one thing is identified with another, such as when Hamlet calls his father a "fair mountain." (See also **simile**.)

monologue—a speech delivered by a single character.

motif—a recurrent theme or image, such as disease in *Hamlet* or moonlight in *A Midsummer Night's Dream*.

oxymoron—a phrase that combines two contradictory terms, as in the phrase "sounds of silence" or Hamlet's remark, "I must be cruel only to be kind."

personification—imparting personality to something impersonal ("the sky wept"); giving human qualities to an idea or an inanimate object, as in the saying "love is blind."

pun—a playful treatment of words that sound alike, or are exactly the same, but have different meanings. In *Romeo and Juliet* Mercutio says, after being fatally wounded, "Ask for me tomorrow and you shall find me a grave man." "Grave" could mean either a place of burial or serious.

simile—a figure of speech in which one thing is compared to another, usually using the word *like* or *as*. (See also **metaphor**.)

soliloquy—a speech delivered by a single character, addressed to the audience. The most famous are those of Hamlet, but Shakespeare uses this device frequently to tell us his characters' inner thoughts.

symbol—a visible thing that stands for an invisible quality, as poison in *Hamlet* stands for evil and treachery.

syntax—sentence structure or grammar. Shakespeare displays amazing variety of syntax, from the sweet simplicity of his songs to the clotted fury of his great tragic heroes, who can be very difficult to understand at a first hearing. These effects are deliberate; if we are confused, it is because Shakespeare means to confuse us.

theme—the abstract subject or message of a work of art, such as revenge in *Hamlet* or overweening ambition in *Macbeth*.

tone—the style or approach of a work of art. The tone of *A Midsummer Night's Dream*, set by the lovers, Bottom's crew, and the fairies, is light and sweet. The tone of *Macbeth*, set by the witches, is dark and sinister.

tragedy—a story that traces a character's fall from power, sanity, or privilege. Shakespeare's well-known tragedies include *Hamlet, Macbeth*, and *Othello*.

tragicomedy—a story that combines elements of both tragedy and comedy, moving a heavy plot through twists and turns to a happy ending.

verisimilitude—having the appearance of being real or true.

understatement—a statement expressing less than intended, often with an ironic or comic intention; the opposite of hyperbole.

SHAKESPEARE AND
HENRY IV, PART 1

Part IV

THE LIFE

OF

SIR JOHN FALSTAFF.

ILLUSTRATED BY GEORGE CRUIKSHANK.

WITH A BIOGRAPHY OF THE KNIGHT, FROM AUTHENTIC SOURCES,

BY

ROBERT B. BROUGH, ESQ.

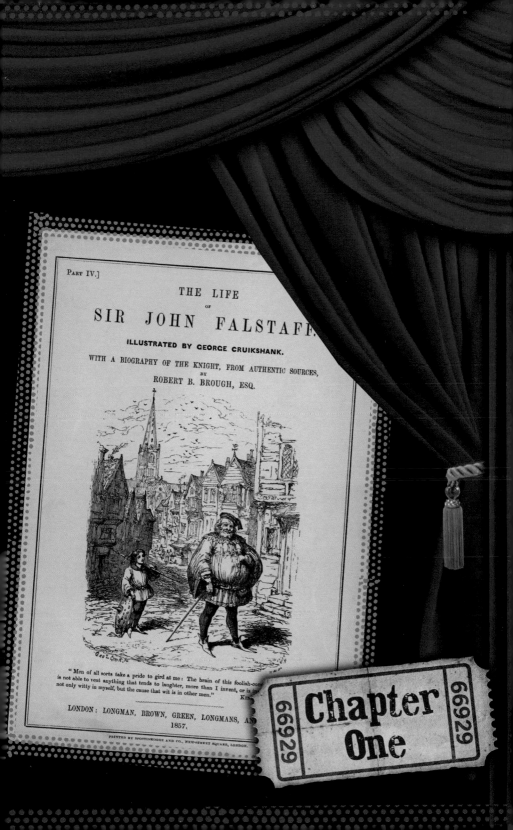

"Men of all sorts take a pride to gird at me: The brain of this foolish-com-
is not able to vent anything that tends to laughter, more than I invent, or is in
not only witty in myself, but the cause that wit is in other men."

Kir

LONDON: LONGMAN, BROWN, GREEN, LONGMANS, AN
1857.

PRINTED BY SPOTTISWOODE AND CO., NEW-STREET SQUARE, LONDON.

CHAPTER ONE

Shakespeare and Henry IV, Part 1

HENRY IV, PART 1 IS WIDELY REGARDED AS ONE OF SHAKESPEARE'S SUPREME ACHIEVEMENTS A MATCHLESS BLEND OF HISTORY, COMEDY, AND TRAGEDY PACKED WITH WONDERFUL CHARACTERS, EXCITING DRAMA, AND UNFORGETTABLE ELOQUENCE. IT HAS BEEN ONE OF SHAKESPEARE'S MOST POPULAR PLAYS SINCE ITS FIRST APPEARANCE. IT IS AMAZINGLY RICH IN LIFE, AND IT FEATURES PERHAPS THE MOST HILARIOUS CREATION IN ENGLISH LITERATURE, SIR JOHN FALSTAFF.

The play, with its sequels (*Henry IV, Part 2* and *Henry V*), and with *Richard II* as its prologue, retells the legend of Henry V, the prodigal son who abandoned his wild ways and became a mighty king. It does this with a brilliant gallery of characters: King Henry IV; his son, Prince Hal; the lovable rebel Hotspur; the Welsh wizard Owen Glendower; characters such as Mistress Quickly, hostess of the tavern; and, of course, the eternally appealing reprobate knight Falstaff, who steals the show. (Many scholars believe that it was this character's appeal to the Elizabethan audience that forced Shakespeare to write the second part of *Henry IV*, which, in many ways, seems merely to duplicate the first part. For example, Prince Hal redeems himself in his father's eyes all over again. It seems a little superfluous!)

Nearly all these characters have proved to be complex enough to inspire debate among readers, who argue over whether Henry IV and his son are legitimate kings and whether the final banishment of Falstaff, the great favorite of every generation of spectators, is necessary and justified. The play illustrates Shakespeare's imaginative power and his ability to keep producing an inexhaustible line of characters about whom it has been said that "it is possible to have next to the last word on them, but never the last."

The whole cycle of Shakespeare's Henry V plays invites us to meditate on the nature of kingship, on political right and wrong, and on the relations between power and human nature. To whom do we owe loyalty? And what do rulers owe to the people they rule? Do the usual rules of morality apply to those who bear responsibility for entire nations?

Of course even Shakespeare cannot give us the answers to such enduring questions, but he does make us feel their force as no other dramatist has done. The fictitious persons in his mind have a vividness and poignancy that seems superior to that of the real people we encounter in the records of history and even, for the most part, in our own personal experience. To read Shakespeare is to enter a world that is higher than our own, and one we never want to leave once we have been there.

In the Henry V plays, we may be repelled by Hal's conscious plan to make friends whom he will later discard after they have served his purpose. Hal announces this intention to us in his first and only soliloquy, at the end of his first scene with Falstaff, for whom he shows very little affection throughout the whole tetralogy (group of four plays). We come to love this huge, fun-loving, and big-hearted knight, but Hal never really does, and we are shocked when he finally snubs and humiliates the old man, who cherishes him as dearly as a son, in a public procession.

Many readers take the view that Falstaff, by greeting the new Henry V so intimately in public (calling him "my sweet boy"), has crossed a line of familiarity that no king can afford to allow to be violated if he values his dignity and the respect of his people. But for others, the banishment of Falstaff is the most infamous act of Henry's kingship, a personal betrayal that cannot be excused on grounds of statesmanship.

Such an argument can never be settled. *Henry IV* shows why it is so hard to speak definitively of Shakespeare's creations. There are always more angles to be considered and more things to be said. And this inexhaustible quality gives us endless delight.

Henry IV, Part 1 is the second (and many would say the most brilliant) play in the great tetralogy of English history, sometimes called Shakespeare's *Henriad*, which begins with the tragic *Richard II*, continues with the two parts of *Henry IV*, and reaches its climax in *Henry V*. (Shakespeare had written another tetralogy earlier in which he covered the aftermath of this one: the three parts of *Henry VI*, followed by *Richard III*.)

Richard II tells the story of Richard's overthrow and death at the hands of his cousin Henry Bolingbroke, Duke of Hereford, who usurped the throne as King Henry IV. The play is full of religious symbols: England is likened to Paradise, and Richard is compared to both Adam and Christ.

All four plays trace the results of Henry's usurpation, chiefly civil wars which make his seizure of the throne a sort of national original sin. These themes were urgent and exciting to Elizabethan audiences, who feared that this bloody history might repeat itself when their aged queen, Elizabeth I. died. (In fact, followers of the Earl of Essex staged a performance of *Richard II* in 1601, hoping to incite rebellion, and Essex himself was beheaded in that same year for trying to depose the queen. In Shakespeare's day, civil war was by no means a remote possibility.)

Near the end of *Richard II*, King Henry learns to his distress that his son

Henry, the prince who will later rule as Henry V, has become notorious for frequenting London's taverns and brothels with his "unrestrained loose companions." He is reportedly "dissolute" and "desperate."

Shakespeare is setting the stage for his treatment of one of England's national legends: the startling transformation of the wild and irresponsible Prince Hal into the heroic King Henry V, glorious conqueror of France. The metamorphosis begins in the first part of *Henry IV*, continues in the second part, and is completed in *Henry V*. Echoes of the story of Adam's fall recur throughout the *Henriad*.

Not everyone agrees that Prince Hal's maturation into a king is a change for the better; many readers see him as a cold and calculating hypocrite, like his cynical father. Once again Shakespeare creates a three-dimensional character who is not easy to judge. But however we evaluate him, he remains the central figure in Shakespeare's most ambitious dramatic sequence.

The language of *Henry IV, Part 1* presents special problems, and no student should feel intimidated by them. The play deals with complex historical events, situations, and relations of kinship, and it is also full of Elizabethan slang words, especially in the scenes where Falstaff appears. Once these are mastered, the story line and the humor become much easier to follow. (As always, a good professional performance on stage, film, or recording, will clarify many difficulties and convey the rhythm of Shakespeare's language.)

THE PLAY'S THE THING

- OVERVIEW AND
  ANALYSIS

- LIST OF CHARACTERS

- ANALYSIS OF MAJOR
  CHARACTERS

A frontispiece to ▶
the score of Verdi's
opera *Falstaff*, first
performed in 1893

Chapter Two

66929

The Play's the Thing

ACT I, SCENE 1

OVERVIEW

King Henry, sick of civil war in England, expresses to his lords his determination to bring peace to his country and repeats his resolution (made in the final scene of *Richard II*) to make a pilgrimage to the Holy Land. But the Earl of Westmoreland has bad news for him: The Welsh rebel Owen Glendower has captured Lord Edmund Mortimer (a kinsman of the late Richard II and thus a possible rival claimant to the throne) and has slaughtered a thousand of his men, horribly mutilating their corpses. Henry remarks that this act of violence will force him to abandon his plan to visit the Holy Land. Westmoreland adds further troubling news: The gallant young Henry Percy, known by the nickname Hotspur, has been fighting Scottish rebels, but the outcome is still unknown. Henry, however, has heard the result: Hotspur has won the battle and taken many prisoners. When Westmoreland remarks that this is "a conquest for a prince to boast of," Henry answers sadly that Hotspur's valor reminds him, by contrast, of how wild his own son is. Hotspur refuses to yield most of his prisoners to King Henry. Westmoreland blames this defiance on Hotspur's uncle, the Earl of Worcester, who has always been Henry's enemy. The king agrees. He must have it out with both men.

ANALYSIS

No sooner has Henry assumed the throne that he usurped from Richard II than he faces a new set of problems. Not everyone accepts his right to rule. Potential rebels are everywhere, and some of the lords he thinks should be his subjects reject his authority. To make matters worse, his own son Henry—or Prince Hal, as his friends call him—is misbehaving notoriously.

As he does so often, Shakespeare, for dramatic purposes, takes great liberties with the facts of history. The real Hotspur was nearly a generation older than Prince Hal, but Shakespeare was inspired to make them about the same age so that they could be evenly matched rivals. This opposition also makes Hal's disreputable and dishonorable conduct all the more painful to his father.

OVERVIEW

Prince Hal exchanges sharp but good-natured barbs, puns, and other jokes with his obese, witty friend Sir John ("Jack") Falstaff. Falstaff not only addresses the prince by his first name, but uses the familiar pronouns *thou* and *thee* instead of such formalities as *your majesty*. In addition, we learn

DAVID WARNER (LEFT) AS FALSTAFF AND GEOFFREY STREATFEILD AS PRINCE HAL SHARE A SCENE IN THE 2008 ROYAL SHAKESPEARE COMPANY PRODUCTION.

that Hal pays for their tavern entertainment, both in cash and in credit. Falstaff says he will change his sinful ways, but as soon as Hal proposes that they commit a robbery, he is eager to join in.

Their friend Ned Poins arrives, and after he and Hal tease Falstaff together, Ned names the site and time where they may rob some "pilgrims going to Canterbury with rich offerings and traders riding to London with fat purses": at Gadshill at four o'clock the next morning. Hal and Falstaff agree to this, and Falstaff the fat knight departs.

As soon as Falstaff is gone, Poins proposes a practical joke: He and Hal, failing to show up as promised, will let Falstaff, Bardolph, Peto, and Gadshill (also the name of another crony) commit the robbery, and then, in disguise, will rob the robbers.

Hal is delighted with this plan. The best part of the joke, Poins says, will be to meet the "fat rogue" at supper time, to ask him how the robbery went, and then to listen to the outrageous lies he is sure to tell.

Left alone, Hal reveals his own ultimate plan to us in a soliloquy. For a while, he tells us, he will continue to keep company with these lowlife rascals, allowing the world to think he is no better than they are. But finally, he says, he will "imitate the sun," casting them off and seeming to make a dazzling reformation like the sun bursting gloriously through clouds, mists, and fogs.

ANALYSIS

In this scene we see a comic aspect of the anarchy with which King Henry must deal: his son's apparent descent into the criminal world of London.

First we meet Sir John Falstaff, one of Shakespeare's greatest characters, and surely the wittiest. Although he is totally given over to a sinful life, he makes a joke of it by continually quoting the Bible, promising to reform, and even blaming Hal for corrupting him. Tongue in cheek, he says that

Hal is:

> INDEED ABLE TO CORRUPT A SAINT. THOU HAST DONE
> MUCH HARM UPON ME, HAL, GOD FORGIVE THEE FOR IT.
> BEFORE I KNEW THEE, HAL, I KNEW NOTHING. AND NOW
> AM I, IF A MAN SHOULD SPEAK TRULY, LITTLE BETTER
> THAN ONE OF THE WICKED. I MUST GIVE OVER THIS LIFE,
> AND I WILL GIVE IT OVER. BY THE LORD, AN I DO NOT,
> I AM A VILLAIN. I'LL BE DAMNED FOR NEVER A
> KING'S SON IN CHRISTENDOM.

Here is the first full blast of Falstaff's humor. What Hamlet is to tragedy, Falstaff is to comedy. Notice that his joking around is heavily theological: He speaks of grace and damnation, saints and forgiveness, and he stands all Christian doctrine on its head. He also reverses the common opinion that he has debauched the young prince by pretending that it is the young prince who has seduced the old sinner. With boundless effrontery, he plays the innocent, in a parody of a preacher.

When Hal taunts him for joining a robbery immediately after promising to amend his life, Falstaff is ready with an instant, pseudo-scriptural retort: Robbery is his calling! "Why, Hal, 'tis my vocation, Hal. 'Tis no sin for a man to labor in his vocation." It is no use trying to trap this man verbally: He always escapes, mockingly adopting the voice of authority to make it all sound reasonable. His friends take as much delight in these antics as he does.

Still Hal and Poins think they can embarrass Falstaff with a trick: They will let him commit the robbery at Gadshlll without them, then entangle him in the gross lies that he is sure to tell about it afterward.

The scene ends with Hal's self-disclosure: His friendship with Falstaff and the others is a sham. Later, when he rejects them, the world will think he has made an amazing reformation. Readers still debate whether his premeditated duplicity is justified.

ACT 1, SCENE 3

During a meeting with several lords, King Henry has his showdown with the hostile Percys: Thomas Percy, Earl of Worcester; his brother Henry Percy, Earl of Northumberland; and Henry's son, the younger Henry Percy, known as Hotspur.

The king is furious. He says he will now demand the respect that he deserves but has failed to receive. When Worcester insolently answers that his house does not merit such treatment from the man it has helped raise to the throne, King Henry orders him to be gone. The angry Worcester leaves the room.

Northumberland pleads that his son Hotspur has been wrongly accused of denying his prisoners to the king, particularly Mortimer. Hotspur says he never meant to deny them, but was so exasperated at the end of the battle by the king's messenger, a foppish lord, that he is unsure what he said to the demand. Sir Walter Blunt argues that whatever Hotspur said in the heat of the moment must be excused, as long as he retracts it now.

But, the king objects, Hotspur is still withholding those prisoners, with the proviso that he, King Henry, pay a ransom for Hotspur's brother-in-law "the foolish Mortimer," Earl of March, who betrayed the men he led to the Welsh magician Glendower. In short, the king says, Mortimer is a traitor.

THE BLOOD MORE STIRS TO ROUSE A LION THAN TO START A HARE!

Hotspur, who is married to Mortimer's sister, is enraged and defends Mortimer. He recalls that Mortimer fought bravely and suffered many wounds for King Henry's sake, even in single combat with Glendower.

The king says Hotspur is lying: Mortimer would never have dared to fight Glendower. Henry commands Hotspur to stop speaking of Mortimer and to send all the prisoners he has captured to the king. With the clear threat of revenge if Hotspur disobeys, Henry departs with his train of loyal followers.

Now Hotspur, always quick-tempered, is beside himself: "And if the devil come and roar for them, / I will not send them." As his father tries to calm him, his uncle Worcester returns. Hotspur keeps ranting, pledging to fight to his last drop of blood to make Mortimer king. He remarks that the very name of Mortimer makes King Henry look pale and tremble. Worcester and Northumberland agree that Richard II had named him "the next of blood" and that he, not the usurping Henry, is therefore England's rightful king.

Now Hotspur is on a roll. He rails against the king, reiterates his support for Mortimer, and dwells at length on the theme of honor, which he equates with military glory. (Later in the play, Falstaff will offer a very different philosophy of honor.) There is no shutting him up, as he himself good-humoredly acknowledges; he can see the funny side of his own nature. But when he finally calms down, the three men plot the overthrow of Henry Bolingbroke, also known as King Henry IV.

ANALYSIS

King Henry decides that the time has come to settle beyond doubt the question of who is the boss in England. He makes uncompromising demands for the prisoners Hotspur has taken, especially Mortimer. He shows that he is no weakling by deliberately humiliating the three Percys in a way that ensures they will be his enemies.

By the end of their conversation, they hate him bitterly and are resolved to dethrone him and make Mortimer king. Hotspur emerges as the leader of the opposition to King Henry. Shakespeare is already preparing us for the final battle between Hotspur and Hal at the climax of the play.

ACT II, SCENE 1

OVERVIEW

In the wee hours at an inn at Rochester, the servants begin the day by chatting about horses and food. Gadshill, the confederate of the robbers (Falstaff, Peto, and Bardolph), discovers when the travelers plan to set out.

ANALYSIS

This brief scene is self-explanatory.

ACT II, SCENE 2

OVERVIEW

On the highway to Gadshill, Poins has hidden Falstaff's horse, forcing the fat knight to walk. When Falstaff discovers this, he becomes angry and calls loudly for Poins. Hal sharply orders him to hush. When Falstaff keeps muttering and demanding his horse, Hal again tells him bluntly to keep quiet. Gadshill arrives and tells them that the travelers are approaching. Hal and Poins put on their disguises and hide.

Falstaff leads the thieves, ordering the travelers to "stand" (give up their money). Threatening to cut their throats, he pretends in the dark that the robbers are young, shamelessly inveighing against their victims: "They hate us youth! . . . Young men must live." The poor travelers are tied up, robbed, and removed from the scene.

Hal and Poins, wearing buckram (stiff linen or cotton) suits, come on the scene. Then Falstaff and the thieves come back. As Falstaff denounces

Hal and Poins as "cowards" for failing (as he thinks) to show up for the robbery, the two arrive in their disguises and demand the money the thieves have just stolen from the travelers. Most of the thieves flee at once; Falstaff flees after them, leaving the money behind. Hal and Poins seize the booty. Their joke has gone exactly as they planned it.

ANALYSIS

Even when he is committing a capital crime—armed robbery—Falstaff displays his matchlessly aggressive humor, feigning not only youth but also moral indignation against his victims. He habitually assumes the moral high ground and rarely lets anyone put him on the defensive.

ACT II, SCENE 3

OVERVIEW

At his castle in Northumberland, Hotspur is alone, reading a letter from a lord—we are never told his name—who is reluctant to risk taking arms against the king. This timidity (or prudence) angers Hotspur, and he comments with sarcastic wit on every sentence he reads. To his mind, the writer is a hopeless fool and coward.

His wife joins him, remarking on his strange behavior lately: He has shown her no love for a fortnight, talking to himself about military matters and leaving her longing for some sign of affection. Hotspur would rather make war than love. But he refuses to share his thoughts with her. What is on his mind, he tells her, is none of a woman's business. He will not tell her where he is going, but he will allow her to follow him and join him later.

ANALYSIS

In this charming scene, Hotspur shows us both his temper and his warm humor. Despite his fierce scorn for the author of the letter he is reading, he banters lovingly with his wife. He is truly fond of her, but in his world fighting and honor must come first. Though he insists on her obedience, he

treats her with tenderness and
respects her intelligence even as
he teases her.

ACT II,
SCENE 4

OVERVIEW

In the great tavern scene, we see
Falstaff in all his shameless glory,
triumphantly outwitting the trap
Hal has laid for him.

The scene opens with Hal and
Poins teasing Francis, the boy who
serves drinks at the Boar's Head
Tavern in London.

HOTSPUR (OWEN TEALE) AND
LADY PERCY (SYLVESTRA
LE TOUZEL) PERFORMING
AT LONDON'S BARBICAN
THEATER, 1992

Falstaff arrives with Bardolph, Peto, and Gadshill. He is grumbling
about cowards and complaining about the wine having lime in it. As usual
he talks about reforming his life. He accuses Hal and Poins of cowardice.
Hal asks him why he is so upset.

Falstaff proceeds to invent a wild lie about how he and his companions
stole a thousand pounds in a robbery, but then were themselves robbed
of all the money by a gang of a hundred men. Hal eggs him on, pressing him
for details. Falstaff's story keeps growing more and more preposterous:
He relates how he himself fought with as many as fifty men at once, for
two hours. His facts and numbers keep changing, but Hal lets him go on
ranting, the better to shame him later.

Finally Hal springs his trap. He accuses Falstaff of lying and of
contradicting himself in the plainest details. The two men exchange

FALSTAFF (ROBERT STEPHENS) ENTHRALLS HIS TAVERN MATES WITH A TALL TALE IN A ROYAL SHAKESPEARE COMPANY (RSC) PRODUCTION, 1992.

hearty insults and denials until Hal reveals that the "hundred men" were actually only two—Hal himself and Poins—who watched Falstaff and the other thieves rob the travelers, then easily snatched the loot from them and caused them to run away, as Falstaff "roared for mercy." After giving a precise account of what really happened, Hal demands that the fat rogue explain himself.

Far from being defeated or discouraged, the ever-brazen Falstaff goes on the attack. Citing the myth that "the lion will not touch the true prince," he says he instinctively recognized Hal—and spared his life. "Instinct is a great matter. I was now a coward upon instinct," he asserts, even though "thou knowest I am as valiant as Hercules." He even has the gall to echo the Bible (Matthew 26:41) as he calls for celebration: "Watch tonight, pray tomorrow."

Of course Hal is immensely amused by Falstaff's brilliant evasion of the charge of cowardice, and he at once agrees to the knight's proposal that they improvise a merry play. At this moment Mistress Quickly, hostess of the tavern, tells him that an old courtier (attendant of the royal court), sent by Hal's father, has come to see him, but Hal sends Falstaff to shake him off so that their fun will not be interrupted. When Falstaff leaves the room, Hal asks Peto and Bardolph for more details of the "fight"; they tell him how Falstaff hacked his sword with his dagger and had them make their noses bleed so it would appear to be the blood of their supposed assailants.

Falstaff returns with news from the royal court. Hal must go there in the morning to see his father. Hotspur, Glendower, Mortimer, and others are preparing to wage war against King Henry.

Meanwhile they must spend the evening at play. Hal is sure to be severely scolded by his father for spending time with his low companions, so Falstaff will now impersonate the king, while Hal will "practice an answer" to the rebuke he is bound to get.

Playing the king, Falstaff adopts inflated language to chide Hal for hanging out with low rascals, but he makes one exception: He praises "a goodly portly man" whose "name is Falstaff." "I see virtue in his looks; . . . him keep with, the rest banish."

Now they trade roles. Hal pretends to be his father and launches into a denunciation of "a devil [who] haunts thee in the likeness of an old fat man. . . . Falstaff, that old white-bearded Satan." Falstaff, pretending to be Hal, sings the praises of "sweet Jack Falstaff, kind Jack Falstaff, true Jack

WHAT DOTH GRAVITY OUT OF HIS BED AT MIDNIGHT?

Falstaff, valiant Jack Falstaff, and therefore more valiant being, as he is, old Jack Falstaff, banish not him. . . . Banish plump Jack, and banish all the world." Hal, "pretending" to be himself, answers ominously and prophetically: "I do, I will."

At this point Mistress Quickly, Bardolph, and Francis leave the room as a loud knocking is heard at the door. Mistress Quickly returns to tell Hal that the sheriff and the watchmen have come to search the house. Falstaff, who has a good idea of what they want, hides behind an arras (curtain).

The sheriff arrives with one of the carriers who has been robbed; he apologetically tells Hal that they are seeking "certain men" who are wanted for a robbery, and mentions that they are led by "a gross fat man." Hal assures them that the fat man, whom he employs, is not there, but promises to send him to answer any charges the next day.

When the sheriff and carrier depart, Hal finds Falstaff asleep and snoring behind the arras. In his pockets are receipts for a little food and more than two gallons of sack (sherry wine). Hal tells Peto that they must all get ready for war; he will find Peto an honorable position and procure a company of foot soldiers for Falstaff. Meanwhile, he will more than repay the money that they took in the robbery.

ANALYSIS

This scene shows the essence of Falstaff's humor: boundless effrontery. He lets nothing shame him. He turns even the foiled robbery into a victory, likening himself to Hercules and a lion: Accused of cowardice, he says that he spared Hal's life! As soon as one of his huge lies is exposed, he invents an even bigger one. And, as always, he has his scriptural verses handy, alluding to the Psalms and to St. Matthew's gospel.

When Hal teases him about his enormous girth, Falstaff replies, "When I was about thy years, Hal, I was not an eagle's talent [talon] in the waist; I could have crept into any alderman's thumb ring. A plague of sighing and grief! It blows a man up like a bladder." Poor Falstaff! To hear him tell it, it is a life of hardship, not gluttony, that has made him obese. He is forever playing with words. Absurd self-pity is only one of his many poses. Like Hamlet, he has a mind that is in "perpetual motion" (his own phrase).

Falstaff easily adopts the pompous voice of royalty when he plays at being Hal's father, railing solemnly against Hal's lowlife friends (except himself, that is). When Hal plays his sanctimonious father and Falstaff plays Hal, he switches nimbly to another pose, this time defending himself with scriptural authority, contrasting his own corpulence with "Pharaoh's lean kine" (starving cattle, which exist only in the Pharaoh's prophetic dream; see Chapter 41 of Genesis).

Falstaff is a master of parody who loves all the voices he makes fun of. He can talk like a king, a bishop, a soldier, or any other kind of authority. Although he is a man of considerable breeding and learning, as well as wide experience, he uses these qualities only to amuse himself and others. To his mind, life is for joy.

ACT III, SCENE 1

OVERVIEW

Hotspur, Glendower, Mortimer, and Worcester meet at Glendower's castle in Wales to discuss their plans to defeat King Henry, but their meeting is disrupted by a clash of personalities when Glendower boasts of his magic powers and Hotspur heaps scornful, even sarcastic, skepticism on Glendower's claims. Mortimer and Worcester warn Hotspur not to antagonize Glendower, but the two men keep clashing over details, even over who speaks better English, and Hotspur refuses to be mollified even when Glendower tries to let him have his way. He also speaks of his contempt for poetry, which Glendower loves.

Glendower leaves the room to fetch Lady Mortimer (his daughter) and Lady Percy, both of whom must be told that their husbands are leaving to go to war. When Glendower returns with the two ladies, Mortimer laments that he and his wife cannot converse without an interpreter: "My wife can speak no English, I no Welsh." Hotspur enjoys the Welsh lady's singing, but keeps teasing his own wife; then he leaves. Glendower and Mortimer also prepare to depart.

ANALYSIS

This scene emphasizes Hotspur's quarrelsome, irritable, yet oddly humorous nature. He loves to fight and bicker (even with his allies) as much as Falstaff loves to play. He refuses to back down; he has a positive passion for contradicting everything that others say. Although he professes to have a low regard for poetry, his own personality is poetic.

The proud, boastful, and eccentric Glendower is only a bit less contentious than Hotspur. The two men's inability to get along does not bode well for their rebellion against King Henry. In the end, everyone has to appease Hotspur.

ACT III, SCENE 2

OVERVIEW

Hal goes to see his father, who dismisses all his lords so that they can talk alone. The king proceeds to scold his wayward son, whom, he says, heaven has inflicted on him to punish him for his sins. Hal admits that his own life has been far from blameless, but he begs the king to forgive him and not to believe all the malicious rumors he may have heard.

King Henry readily pardons his son, but then recalls how differently he himself used to behave. Unlike Hal, who has made himself a common and contemptible figure in public, King Henry kept out of sight so that people marveled at his rare appearances and he was even more popular than King Richard II himself. In fact, he says, Richard, like Hal, lost the respect of the people by becoming too familiar. This reflection causes his eyes to fill with tears. Hal is moved and promises to mend his ways and to recover his dignity as a prince.

King Henry presses the comparison between Hal and Richard further. Just as Hal is acting as Richard did, Hotspur, he says, is behaving as he, King Henry, did, winning men's sympathy and applause and even threatening to capture the throne itself. The king adds bitterly that he need say no more about his enemies, since Hal himself has, in effect, become his foe and might as well be paid by Hotspur, who is fighting for King Henry's overthrow.

This is too much for Hal. He begs his father to banish these thoughts and to think well of him; he vows to redeem himself, and promises that he will defeat Hotspur in single combat if he ever gets the chance to do so.

His words—"A hundred thousand rebels die in this!"—cheer up the king immensely. Just at this moment, Sir Walter Blunt arrives with urgent news: The mighty enemy forces have gathered at Shrewsbury for the great battle to unseat King Henry. This challenge rouses the king to a new determination, and he gives instructions for countermeasures.

ANALYSIS

Both Henrys, father and son, are shown to be very tough men, prepared for anything their enemies may spring on them. At last Hal is about to put into effect his plan to amaze the world by appearing to mature suddenly; he is eager to meet the formidable Hotspur head-on. The enemy is ready, too. The civil war incited by Henry's usurpation of Richard II's throne is finally coming to a head.

OVERVIEW

The mercurial Falstaff is in another of his countless unpredictable moods, this time a melancholy one. Since the Gadshill robbery, he tells Bardolph, he has been wasting away. He must repent and return to church before his mood changes again. When Bardolph replies that he must stop worrying, Falstaff agrees and asks for an off-color song to raise his spirits. Bardolph teases him about being so fat, and he answers with biblical jests about Bardolph's nose, which is red because he drinks too much.

As Mistress Quickly arrives, Falstaff asks her whether she has learned who stole a valuable ring out of his pocket while he was asleep behind the arras. This implied (and false) reflection on her house makes her furious, which is what he intends, and he amuses himself by teasing her and Bardolph together. He refuses to take responsibility for the huge bills he has run up.

When the scatter-brained hostess tries to protest that Prince Hal has often said that Falstaff's supposedly precious ring was only copper, Falstaff says Hal is a sneaky rascal whom he would cudgel if he were present. At this very moment, naturally, Hal and Peto arrive together, marching, and Falstaff playfully joins them, asking Hal if their marching means that war is imminent.

The hostess tries to get Hal's attention, but Falstaff keeps cutting her off with his lies, insults, and outlandish accusations; the poor woman can hardly get a word in. When she finally manages to tell Hal the things Falstaff has said and done, Hal scolds Falstaff for abusing her and makes it clear that it was he himself who picked Falstaff's pocket as he slept.

Pretending to be innocent, as always, Falstaff, never missing a beat, tells the hostess that *he* forgives *her*. (Instead of being enraged, the gullible, confused woman is mollified, and departs.) After telling Falstaff he has repaid the money to the travelers they robbed, Hal adds that he has also gotten Fallstaff command of some foot soldiers.

ANALYSIS

Shakespeare displays still more facets of one of his great inexhaustible characters, as Falstaff adopts another mood—one of penitence, complete with his usual mock piety and scriptural learning—and tries to defraud the obtuse hostess of her meager wealth. He talks as rapidly as he thinks. Her mind is no match for his, and he has no scruples whatsoever. It is his utter ruthlessness against this helpless adversary that makes the scene so funny. He has no real cruelty or malice in him; his chief motive is simply to amuse himself with his inventive antics at the expense of whoever happens to be handy—whether it is Bardolph, Mistress Quickly, or Prince Hal. At the end of the scene, we learn that he will play a role in the civil war, commanding a troop of infantry—which will offer him one more comic opportunity.

ACT IV, SCENE 1

OVERVIEW

Encamped near Shrewsbury, Hotspur, Worcester, and Douglas (the Scot) are preparing for war. Just then a messenger brings a letter from Hotspur's father, Northumberland, saying that he is seriously ill and will be unable to join them.

Hotspur is angry: The timing of his father's illness is obviously very bad. He tries to be brave about it, but Worcester argues that it may have grave results: Northumberland's absence will discourage the rebel forces, who will suspect that he is missing on purpose. It will also breed doubt about whether the rebels' cause is just.

Again Hotspur looks for a bright side. If the rebels can fight well even without his father and his forces, he argues, men will come to the

conclusion that, with him, they might have captured the kingdom.

Sir Richard Vernon brings more news. The Earl of Westmoreland, with Prince John (Hal's younger brother), is approaching with seven thousand troops; the king is also coming in person with even more forces. When Hotspur asks whether Hal, the "madcap Prince of Wales," is coming, Vernon describes him as so splendidly armed that Hotspur cuts him off in irritation. He is eager to meet Hal in combat, "hot horse to horse," until one of them is dead.

Vernon has more ominous news: Glendower cannot bring his army for another fourteen days. So the rebels will have to face King Henry's armies with serious disadvantages on their side. Hotspur still tries to talk bravely, but now he is speaking not of victory but of glorious death.

ANALYSIS

It is becoming clear that the rebels' cause is collapsing. All the news they receive is dispiriting. Meanwhile every indication is that fortune favors King Henry. By the end of the scene even Hotspur is no longer optimistic; he merely hopes for the glory of slaying Prince Hal in single combat.

We are apt to overlook this in the rush of events. Hotspur's mind is so concentrated on his own honor that he forgets the cause he is supposedly fighting for: installing Mortimer as the rightful king of England.

ACT IV, SCENE 2

OVERVIEW

On their way to battle, Falstaff, now an infantry captain, tries to beg a bottle of sack from Bardolph. Left alone, he tells us his dubious scheme for making money: He conscripts men who can afford to buy their way out of service, pockets the money, then fills their places with sorry substitutes whom he describes as "scarecrows." Prince Hal arrives with the Earl of Westmoreland and, seeing Falstaff's troops, comments, "I did never see such pitiful rascals." Westmoreland agrees that they are "too beggarly." The prince urges Falstaff to follow them quickly to the impending battle, but once the nobles leave, the fat knight says he hopes that he'll arrive there too late too fight but just in time for the victory feast.

ANALYSIS

We meet Falstaff at his most cynical and unfeeling in this scene. He represents the underside of war, with all its greed and indifference to life, and, for once, he is hardly amusing. We must beware of being distracted and seduced by his humor.

What is funny is not the same thing as what is morally right, or forgivable. Shakespeare never forgets the crucial difference. Here the play becomes a bitter satire of war, which makes Falstaff's cold calculation seem rational.

ACT IV, SCENE 3

OVERVIEW

Hotspur and the other rebel leaders debate when they should commence fighting with the king's armies. Sir Walter Blunt arrives with a peace offering from the king, and Hotspur receives him courteously, with respect and love, wishing they could all be on the same side. His regret shows that in spite of all his hunger for military honor, even he is touched by the pathos and tragedy of this war.

Blunt gets to the point: King Henry is willing to redress any just grievances the rebels have, and to pardon their rebellion.

Hotspur answers with sarcasm:

He recalls that Henry owes his crown to Hotspur, his father, and his uncle, who helped him when he was weak and friendless, a "poor unminded outlaw sneaking home" from exile abroad and asking only to have his title as Duke of Lancaster restored. Gradually Henry made himself popular, pretending to be concerned only for his country's sufferings until he was able to depose King Richard and have him killed, taking the throne and also depriving Mortimer of his just claim to the crown.

Nevertheless he tells Blunt that he will send Worcester with an answer the next day. Peace is not ruled out.

ANALYSIS

Both sides are aware that this civil war is a tragedy. It was not necessary; its causes were—and still are—arbitrary. Peace is still possible, if only the stubborn combatants can abandon the pride and resentment that drove them to fight. But, as in every feud, wrongs accumulate until revenge becomes the chief motive of both parties.

ACT IV, SCENE 4

OVERVIEW

Far from the scene of battle, the Archbishop of York and Sir Michael, both of whom favor the rebels, discuss the growing odds against them. The archbishop gives Sir Michael letters for their allies he says are urgent and important. But the powers of King Henry appear to have grown nearly invincible.

ANALYSIS

Even the church cannot stay aloof from the war. So much for Christian teaching and peace! Things have come a long way since King Henry resolved, at the beginning of the play, to make a pilgrimage to the Holy Land.

ACT V, SCENE 1

OVERVIEW

Near Shrewsbury, King Henry, Prince Hal, and others hold a meeting with Worcester and Vernon. Worcester protests that he never wanted this war, but reminds the king that he and his family helped Henry when he was friendless and in acute need—only to be deceived by Henry, who had sworn that he sought only to claim his title as Duke of Lancaster. The king replies that these are flimsy pretexts for rebellion.

AN 1881 WOOD ENGRAVING DEPICTS KING HENRY IV, PRINCE HAL, AND PRINCE JOHN OF LANCASTER AS THEY PREPARE TO BATTLE THE REBELS IN ACT V, SCENE 1.

Hal interjects that he has deep respect for Worcester's nephew Hotspur and, in order to save both sides much bloodshed, offers to settle the dispute by meeting him in single combat. The king expresses his great pride in his son, but vetoes this gallant proposal. He offers peace and pardon, and allows the two men to return to their camp and to present his terms to the other rebels. Hal predicts that these will be rejected.

As the others depart, Hal teases Falstaff about his reluctance to fight. Alone, Falstaff delivers his own cowardly credo: "Honor" is a mere word, "air," of no use or value to either the dead or the living—and he intends to live.

ANALYSIS

Can war still be averted? Hal's proposed alternative is to stake everything on a personal battle between Hotspur and himself. Falstaff, for his part, thinks the whole business is nonsense; neither side's cause, he feels, has any claim on him. He speaks for the individual who is caught in the middle between two powerful forces and must somehow look to his own survival.

ACT V, SCENE 2

OVERVIEW

Having returned to the rebel camp, Worcester tells Vernon that Hotspur must not learn of the king's generous terms of peace. When Vernon objects, Worcester argues that even if the king keeps his word for the time being, he will seek a way to punish the rebels later, especially Worcester and Hotspur's father; therefore the truth must be kept from the impetuous Hotspur. Vernon agrees to go along with this lie.

Hotspur, with Douglas, asks for news. Worcester tells him that the king is eager for battle, not mentioning the king's offer of peace. As a result, a challenge is sent to the king. Worcester tells Hotspur that Hal offered

"I WOULD 'TWERE BEDTIME, HAL, AND ALL WELL."

to meet him in single combat. Hotspur is willing, but is annoyed when Worcester keeps praising the prince's admirable and courteous demeanor. He promises to kill Hal before nightfall. The rebel leaders embrace. The battle is about to begin.

ANALYSIS

Now cynicism prevails. Worcester and Vernon choose to deceive their own side, since, they reason, the war will settle nothing in the long run and Hotspur is a fanatic who loves war for its own sake.

And, in fact, Hotspur wants nothing more than to fight Hal and destroy him. At bottom, Worcester and Vernon pretty much share Falstaff's skeptical view of the conflict and military glory.

ACT V, SCENE 3

OVERVIEW

In the battle the Earl of Douglas confronts Sir Walter Blunt, one of several men disguised as the king. When Douglas kills Blunt he mistakenly exults that he has killed King Henry He tells Hotspur that he has killed the king, but Hotspur corrects him, telling him that he has slain Sir Walter Blunt, a "gallant knight," but only one of several decoys dressed as the king.

As they leave, Falstaff enters and recognizes the dead man as Blunt. "There's honor for you," he remarks. He adds that he has led his "ragamuffins" into a massacre: "There's not three of my hundred and fifty left alive, and they are for the town's end, to beg during life."

Hal finds Falstaff and tells him to lend him his sword, since he has lost his. Falstaff replies that he must rest from his day's feats in battle; he says that he has slain Hotspur, for one thing. Hal doubts this, says Hotspur is alive, and again demands his sword. Falstaff tells him to take his pistol instead. Hal grabs it, but finds that it is not actually a pistol; it is a bottle of sack! Snapping that this is no time for foolery, he throws the bottle at Falstaff and moves on. Falstaff, alone once more, resolves to save his own hide if he can: "I like not such grinning honor as Sir Walter hath." He concludes, "Give me life, which if I can save, so; if not, honor comes unlooked for, and there's an end."

ANALYSIS

Falstaff's view of war as a series of absurd accidents, accompanied by empty bluster, seems to be borne out by events. Sir Walter Blunt's gallant fighting for King Henry earns him only the reward of a sudden death—the same grim fate that nearly all of Falstaff's poor "ragamuffins" have met. There is no proportion between worth and glory, so why not stay alive and lie about one's military feats, as the braggart Falstaff does? Even honor, "unlooked for," is an accident, one he hopes to avoid if he can.

ACT V, SCENE 4

OVERVIEW

Seeing that Hal is wounded, the king tells him and his brother John to withdraw from the fighting. But Hal praises John's unexpected valor, and the two brothers charge back into battle.

Hal returns to find Douglas attacking his father; he saves the king's life by assailing Douglas, who flees. Henry thanks his son, salutes his courage, and leaves the field just as Hotspur arrives.

Hal and Hotspur identify themselves. Hal pays his respects to this "very valiant rebel," but warns him that he is about to lose his glorious reputation as a warrior. Hotspur retorts with his own threat. They fight, with Falstaff cheering Hal on. Douglas returns and attacks Falstaff, who falls as if he is dead. Douglas exits.

Hal kills Hotspur and delivers a gallant eulogy for the brave rebel. Seeing Falstaff lying on the ground, he thinks he is dead, too, and speaks a brief farewell, but as soon as he leaves, Falstaff gets up, still very much alive. He decides he will claim to have slain Hotspur and picks up the corpse after stabbing it in the leg.

Just then Hal returns with his brother John, whose bravery in battle he is lauding. Both are startled to find Falstaff alive. The fat knight, shameless as ever, deplores falsehood ("Lord, Lord, how this world is given to lying") and explains that he and Hotspur both rose up together and fought for "a long hour by Shrewsbury clock" until he at last slew the rebel. He says he expects to receive a title for this heroic achievement: "I look to be either earl or duke, I can assure you."

The incorrigible Falstaff, alone again, looks forward to his reward. He resolves to lose weight and mend his ways: He will stop drinking and "live cleanly as a nobleman should do."

ANALYSIS

With his defeat of Hotspur, Hal has finally earned the honor he has secretly coveted all along. He has shown real courage and prowess as a warrior, winning his father's joyous approval. He feels real regret when he thinks Falstaff has been killed, but his days of carousing in the taverns of London are over now.

Still he is happy to find his old companion alive after all and up to his old tricks, claiming credit for the death of Hotspur and demanding a title for his valiant feats of arms. In his typical style the obese old knight forms a noble resolution to change his life and to live out his days with the dignity befitting the duke or earl he expects to become. Somehow this is not very convincing. We know that Falstaff, whatever he may say now, will never change.

ACT V, SCENE 5

OVERVIEW

King Henry rejoices over his forces' victory. He condemns Worcester and Vernon for lying to their own side about his offer of peace and orders both men to be put to death. Then he asks Hal for details of the battle.

Hal tells him that Douglas tried to escape, but was captured and is now being held in Hal's tent. He asks his father's permission to dispose of him, which the king readily grants.

Hal generously directs his brother John to release Douglas without ransom, in honor of the high qualities he has shown even in rebellion. King Henry looks forward to making war on the remaining rebels, chiefly Glendower and Mortimer, who are in Wales.

ANALYSIS

"Thus ever did rebellion find rebuke," King Henry says. He is so smug in his victory that he seems to forget the obvious fact that he got his own crown by rebelling against a legitimate king.

Still he looks forward to crushing what is left of this "rebellion"—that is, to completing and consolidating his usurpation, as if that will make his royal line legitimate. But his cloud of guilt will hover over him and, later, over Hal and Hal's son, Henry VI. The Bolingbroke dynasty is destined to have a short historical life.

LIST OF CHARACTERS

King Henry IV, formerly Henry Bolingbroke, Duke of Lancaster

Henry, Prince of Wales, his son and heir apparent
to the throne, nicknamed Hal and Harry

Prince John of Lancaster, younger brother of Prince Henry

Earl of Westmoreland, kinsman and ally of the king

Sir Walter Blunt, standard-bearer for the king

Thomas Percy, Earl of Worcester, enemy of the king

Henry Percy, Earl of Northumberland, his brother

Henry (or Harry) Percy, his son, nicknamed Hotspur,
fiery leader of the rebels

Edmund Mortimer, Earl of March and rival claimant to the throne

Richard Scroop, Archbishop of York and ally of the rebels

Archibald, Earl of Douglas, leader of the Scottish rebels

Owen Glendower, father-in-law of Mortimer
and leader of the Welsh rebels

Sir Richard Vernon, another rebel

Sir Michael, a knight or priest of the archbishop's household

Sir John Falstaff, companion of Prince Henry

Edward (Ned) Poins, gentleman-in-waiting to Prince Henry

Gadshill, setter for the robbers

Peto, crony of Falstaff

Bardolph, another crony of Falstaff

Francis, apprentice tapster

Vintner of the tavern

Lady Percy, called Kate, wife of Hotspur

Lady Mortimer, wife of Mortimer and daughter of Glendower

Mistress Quickly, hostess of the tavern

Carriers, messengers, soldiers, ostlers, chamberlain, travelers, sheriff, lords, attendants, servants

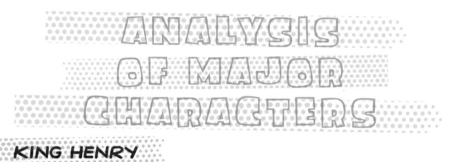

ANALYSIS OF MAJOR CHARACTERS

KING HENRY

Although he is a usurper, Henry IV is one of Shakespeare's ablest rulers. He has seized the throne from the hapless Richard II and is determined not to repeat his predecessor's mistakes. He is shrewd, courageous, and tough, a strong masculine figure.

Yet his reign is far from a happy one. His aloof personality prevents him from forging close bonds with others, either potential allies or his own sons. Nobody really loves him. Power is his only passion. Haunted by the guilt of having overthrown a legitimate king, he is dominated by his fierce ambition. He wants his son and namesake to succeed him and to be accepted by his subjects as legitimate, but Hal's wild ways threaten this hope.

In addition, he must deal with the armed resistance of the formidable forces who refuse to accept him as their monarch and who are resolved to fight for the right of the Earl of March, Edmund Mortimer, to rule. (Mortimer was said to be Richard's personal choice to succeed him.) Uniting the deeply divided kingdom Henry has plucked from Richard will prove a huge task when he must overcome such daunting warriors as the Scottish Earl of Douglas, the fiery young Henry Hotspur, and the uncanny Welsh magician Owen Glendower.

In order to understand how differently people in the Elizabethan era (and in most earlier times) would have seen these matters, we must try to perform a difficult mental adjustment. This early view is hard for us even to imagine now.

In the modern world, the word *rebel* has a certain glamour attached to it, but in Shakespeare's time, rebellion was seen as a sin against the proper and divinely established order of things. Political rebellion in particular was viewed as a crime, unless the supposed rebel could show that he had a better claim to authority than the actual ruler. All authority was believed to come from above, ultimately from God, not from the common people, and almost nobody believed in democracy of any sort.

On this view the common people were considered "rabble," unfit to rule themselves and duty-bound to obey their betters, the rulers God had anointed to supervise them. These "anointed" rulers were, in turn, answerable to God and divine law. It was not that their powers were dictatorial; the dichotomy that we see between democracy and dictatorship did not exist. Christian kings were bound by God's eternal law and could not change it at their whim.

So Henry's political problem is that he, unlike Mortimer, can produce no title to authority. In that sense *he* is the rebel, or, as Hotspur calls him, a "vile politician" with no right to rule England. All he has is raw power, even if he insists that he is the country's rightful king.

Of course Henry's sobriety—even severity—and his concentration on power make him the polar opposite of the devil-may-care Falstaff. He lacks even the faintest trace of charm, and we never wonder that Prince Hal looks elsewhere for companionship. Henry's political shrewdness,

keen as it is, is not matched by moral wisdom. Nobody would call him a very "fatherly" father; Falstaff offers Hal far more warmth as well as fun, so we understand why Hal chooses to spend his time with the dissipated old knight instead of his mirthless sire, whom he avoids.

As a Christian king, Henry hopes to lead an English army to fight infidels in the Holy Land. But this pious aspiration is delayed by the civil war he must contend with and is never fulfilled. (He has been assured by a prophecy that he will die in Jerusalem, which he naturally takes to mean that he will end his days in the Holy Land, but in the second part of *Henry IV*, he falls ill and dies in the Jerusalem chamber at Westminster, thus fulfilling the prophecy in an ironical way.)

PRINCE HAL

Contrary to appearances and his reputation, Hal is highly conscious of his status as heir apparent to the throne. Like Hamlet, he feels he must submit to his father's wishes as a matter of honor.

Even in his carousing with Falstaff and his crew, he always remembers that as a future king of England he must conduct himself with a certain dignity. This awareness prevents him from giving his heart fully to anyone else. Emotionally he is always holding something in reserve. As Laertes says of Hamlet, his choices are "circumscribed" by his royalty.

This does not prevent him from taking real delight in the tavern antics. He loves the fat knight's wit, but he never abandons his self-control or forgets his duty to be worthy of his father. His imagination is fixed on the coming showdown with the rebels, especially his personal battle with Hotspur.

All along, then, Hal leads a double life, which he keeps concealed from Falstaff and the others (until he becomes King Henry V and abruptly repudiates them in Part 2 of *Henry IV*). He has both a fun-loving side and a cold-blooded, priggish one. Like his father, Hal is a skillful pretender. He returns very little of the love Falstaff has for him.

Yet others are struck by his gallantry, modesty, and graciousness, which seem to be heartfelt; he has no illusions about himself, and certainly his high regard for the dashing and charismatic Hotspur is sincere. (He expresses it for the last time, after all, when he is alone with the man's corpse.)

In *The Meaning of Shakespeare*, Harold Goddard makes the provocative contention that Hal is one of several Shakespearean heroes who succumb to the disastrous influence of their fathers. For Goddard, the tragic error is to obey force, personified by Henry IV, rather than imagination, represented (albeit in a highly flawed way) by Falstaff. Seen in this light, Hal is by no means an ideal ruler, and his metamorphosis into a strong king and imperial conqueror cannot be judged very favorably.

HOTSPUR

With his colorful personality—his fierce courage, his boundless appetite for honor, his lack of guile, and his tender, humorous concern for his wife—Hotspur is among Shakespeare's most attractive characters, always a favorite of audiences when he is played well. In their different ways, he, Hal, and Falstaff all illustrate the adage that "the style is the man."

And, like many Shakespearean characters, he is a man of contradictions, although his motives are simple. He may be a brilliant speaker, but his tongue keeps running out of control in spite of his attempts to curb it: We can only smile when he says (in all sincerity) that "I profess not talking." He is helplessly eloquent.

Hotspur is incapable of deceit or double-dealing, and he despises the Machiavellian schemer King Henry IV in large part for his hypocrisy. As he says, this king knows very well when to promise and when to pay. Hotspur is explosive and magnetic; everyone trusts him to keep his word, and even his enemies (including both the king and Prince Hal) salute his gallant nature. His death in battle, though perhaps inevitable given his fearless temper, leaves the world poorer. But he refuses to see any difference between reasonable prudence and mere cowardice. He is also incapable of hesitation.

Although Hotspur is by no means a villain, he has something in common with most of Shakespeare's villains (we may think of Cassius in *Julius Caesar* and Shylock in *The Merchant of Venice*): He professes to detest poetry and music, regarding them as idle and effeminate amusements. This attitude fuels the tension and even hostility between him and the Welsh magician Glendower, and it may be part of the reason, as some critics have argued, for Glendower's disastrous failure to show up with his army at the decisive moment at the field of Shrewsbury.

Here is a case where Shakespeare takes liberties with his historical sources for dramatic effect. The real Hotspur was far older than Prince Henry—roughly a quarter of a century, in fact—but the Bard makes them the same age so that they can be rivals, contrasted for the sake of the story. In the play, Hotspur is the great warrior whose contempt for the "madcap," tavern-haunting playboy prince sets the stage for their final confrontation in the climactic battle of Shrewsbury. This allows Hal to emerge as a hero and also gives Falstaff a chance to add one more moment of comedy when he pretends to be the man who killed the fearsome Hotspur.

The creative process is mysterious, and it may be that Shakespeare originally conceived Hotspur as the play's villain, but, as often happens, the creation ran away with his creator and developed a charm of his own. Something like this may have happened with Falstaff, too, if Shakespeare first planned for him to play a minor role as a disreputable companion whom the young Hal would have to disown as he matured, only to find the fat knight taking over the play with his unruly genius.

FALSTAFF

With Hamlet, Cleopatra, and Iago, Falstaff has been ranked among Shakespeare's supreme creations—a character of infinite resources, forever surprising us with some new revelation of his nature and outgrowing the very play of which he was supposed to be a small part. As Mark Van Doren puts it, Falstaff has the trait of a great man: Everything he says is both unexpected and yet consistent with everything we know about him.

The noted critic Northrop Frye observed that Falstaff combines several kinds of comic stereotype: Among these are the *miles gloriosus*, or braggart soldier; the Vice of the late medieval morality play; the parasite who lives off others. He also has a gift for bluff and bluster, as well as mimicry and parody. No comic character has ever been so well rounded, so versatile and inexhaustible.

Shakespeare often lets his comic characters make wise and penetrating comments on the main action of the play: The sublime Fool in *King Lear* and Feste in *Twelfth Night* are two excellent examples. But none plays so great a role in his drama as Falstaff does. Falstaff is unique in making the audience care about his fate.

Certainly Falstaff's creator loves him. He is the only one of the Bard's most brilliant characters to appear in three separate plays—the two parts of *Henry IV* and *The Merry Wives of Windsor*—and his death is movingly reported in a fourth, *Henry V*. Obviously he was hugely popular with Elizabethan audiences—and even perhaps with Queen Elizabeth herself: According to one legend, Shakespeare wrote *The Merry Wives* in just two weeks when she expressed a wish to see Falstaff in love! The legend is plausible partly because, by general agreement, *The Merry Wives* is an inferior play, a silly comedy, with an inferior Falstaff who shows little of the comic genius for which he is renowned. This shows that so great a character depends on his context and cannot be simply transplanted from history to farce. At any rate, one play can never be big enough to accommodate him. (We may compare him, in this respect, to a fictional hero such as Sherlock Holmes, another character who vastly outgrew his author's initially modest plans for him.)

A gigantic imaginative figure like Falstaff eludes all our attempts at definition. Van Doren calls him a "universal mimic" with a gift for simulating other voices, especially those of authority. He is expert at taking off the royal, lordly, scholarly, military, and ecclesiastical styles. He knows all the ways important men talk and loves to impersonate them. Among other things, he is a master of rhetoric, and his wit and humor are infectious. "I am not only witty in myself," as he says in Part 2, "but the cause that wit is in other men." His adroitness in retort causes Sister Miriam Joseph to remark in her invaluable study *Shakespeare's Use of the Arts of Language*: "Among Shakespeare's characters Falstaff outdoes all others in employing certain devices of sophistry in defense." He can escape from any verbal trap and, like a Houdini, wriggle out of even the most seemingly fatal situation.

Falstaff speaks in short, repetitive bursts, as if he is always nearly out of breath, and it is largely this that makes his own style so instantly recognizable: "Now, Hal, what time of day is it, lad?" "Indeed, you come near me now, Hal." "By the Lord, thou sayest true, lad." "How now, how now, mad wag?" "Thou hast done much harm upon me, Hal, God forgive thee for it." "If the rascal have not given me medicines to make me love him, I'll be hanged." "I prithee, good Prince Hal, help me to my horse, good king's son." "There's no more valor in that Poins than in a wild duck." "A plague of all cowards!—Give me a cup of sack, rogue!—Is there no virtue extant?" "A bad world, I say." "If they speak more or less than truth, they are villains, and the sons of darkness." "What, art thou mad? Art thou mad? Is not the truth the truth?" "By the Mass, lad, thou sayest true." "Peace, good

pint-pot. Peace, good tickle-brain." "Do I not bate? Do I not dwindle?" "Company, villainous company, hath been the spoil of me." "Thou seest I have more flesh than another man and therefore more frailty." "Tut, tut, good enough to toss; food for powder, food for powder. They'll fill a pit as well as better. Tush, man, mortal men, mortal men."

He huffs and puffs constantly of plagues and rogues and hanging, switching readily from insult to affection. His speech is full of colloquial warmth and energy and he swears freely: by the Lord, by the Mass, by our Lady, by Christ's wounds ("Zounds!") and blood ("Sblood!"). His tongue moves readily from lofty religious and classical topics to homely (and edible) items such as shotten herring, stinking mackerel, bunches of radish, old applejohns, peppercorns, and soused gurnets. Even Shakespeare never created a more distinctive voice than Falstaff's.

In one important sense, Falstaff tries to be a loving father to Hal, who does not feel a corresponding affection for the poor old man and secretly plans all along to cast him aside when he has no more use for him. Falstaff may not have principles, but he certainly does have a heart.

A CLOSER LOOK

- THEMES

- MOTIFS

- SYMBOLS

- LANGUAGE

- INTERPRETING THE PLAY

A movie poster for Orson Welles's ▶
1965 movie, *Chimes at Midnight*,
in which he played Falstaff

Distinguished Company
Breathes Life into
Shakespeare's Lusty Age of

CHIMES AT MIDNIGHT

BARRY SALTZMAN PRESENTS AN ORSON WELLES FILM "FALSTAFF" ("CHIMES AT MIDNIGHT") STARRING
MARGARET RUTHERFORD · JOHN GIELGUD · MARINA VLADY · KEITH BAXTER
RELEASED BY PEPPERCORN-WORMSER, INC.-FILM ENTERPRISES

Chapter Three

66929 66929 66929 66929

CHAPTER
THREE

a Closer Look

THEMES

INFLUENCE OF CHARACTER IN HISTORY

In Shakespeare's day it went without saying that monarchy was the natural form of government. If this seems quaint to us now, we should bear in mind that the American presidency has been evolving toward monarchy from the start, even if the problem of succession is supposed to be settled by periodic elections rather than by heredity (though we may note that being a president's son is a great advantage, even in a democracy).

Critics have observed that Shakespeare is not really interested in the complex workings of history, but rather in chronicling the personalities and actions of the individual men who actually win power and hold it. Living before the age of polls and surveys, Shakespeare's concerns are moral and psychological, rather than, say, economic or demographic.

Henry IV is concerned with the questionable legitimacy of its title character, the king who has usurped his throne from the late Richard II, a weakling of a ruler. Is Henry entitled to rule? He has power, but this is not the same thing as authority, or right by succession. Judgments on this issue still differ. But Henry is well aware that a ruler needs the good will and esteem of his subjects, or what we would call favorable public opinion.

Henry's son, Prince Hal or Harry in this play, was to become the legendary and supposedly heroic King Henry V, who invaded and conquered France with a tiny army and married the French princess Catherine, but whose son, King Henry VI, was unable to keep the empire bequeathed to him. Many saw the tragic reign of Henry VI as the result of his grandfather's sin in taking the throne unlawfully. (The traditional heroic view of the French invasion was presented in Laurence Olivier's film *Henry V*, made to boost English morale during World War II.)

What did Shakespeare himself think of all this? As usual, he does not tell us, and we are left to infer his attitude from the play as best we can. Most commentators agree that he was horrified by anarchy and mob rule, but this does not settle the question of which (if either) side he would have favored in a civil war. He shows us both factions and lets them have their say, just as he lets every individual character speak with maximum eloquence.

THE BETTER PART OF VALOR IS DISCRETION

PLAY OF OPPOSITE CHARACTERIZATIONS

And, of course, Shakespeare is always chiefly interested in the individual, often pairing two of his most brilliant characters against one another, as lovers or as enemies. In *Henry IV* he gives us an abundance of vivid personalities: King Henry himself, Prince Hal, Glendower, Hotspur, and Falstaff. The play teems with men who are all capable of memorable speech at any moment. Shakespeare specializes in the unforgettable.

Although Hal and Hotspur are military rivals, the real "mighty opposites" of Shakespeare's imagination are Hotspur and Falstaff. Each holds a philosophy that rejects the other's. In Hotspur's view, honor is everything—his very reason for living. But to Falstaff, honor is utterly empty—mere "air," a thing for which it is absurd to die. Shakespeare lets both men make their cases with all the power of his magnificent words. He is capable of making one argument seriously, even movingly, and then making the opposite argument hilariously. But there is no doubt that *Henry IV* owed its original tremendous popularity (the play was not only published in quarto but went through more editions than any other Shakespeare play except *Richard III*, which was also reprinted six times) to Falstaff's side-splitting merriment. This created the demand for both a sequel and another comedy, *The Merry Wives of Windsor*.

USE OF RELIGIOUS UNDERTONES

Henry IV may also have a buried religious dimension. It appears that Sir John Falstaff was originally named Sir John Oldcastle, a real historical figure who was burned as a heretic and later (in Elizabethan times) revered as a martyr by Protestants, but that the name was changed when Oldcastle's powerful descendants objected to Shakespeare's humorous treatment of him in the play.

Traces of Falstaff's original identity remain in a few humorous touches. In their first scene together, Prince Hal teasingly addresses Falstaff as

"WHILE YOU LIVE, TELL THE TRUTH AND SHAME THE DEVIL!"

"my old lad of the castle," and the epilogue to Part 2 of the play jokingly promises the audience another sequel by "our humble author" set in France "with Sir John in it, . . . where, for anything I know, Falstaff shall die of a sweat, . . . for Oldcastle died a martyr, and this is not the man."

All this may help explain why, even though Falstaff seems to be an unlikely theologian, *Henry IV* contains so many biblical and theological jokes and references. It also tends to strengthen the suspicion that Shakespeare was attached to the old Catholic order and hostile to any religious innovation. Nobody could mistake Falstaff for a Puritan! His habitual mentions of hanging, however casual and humerous, may be faint echoes of Oldcastle's martyrdom.

Like *Hamlet*, *Henry IV*, in its own way, reflects the religious upheavals and disputes of Shakespeare's day. And the sack-soaked sinful Falstaff, always meaning to amend his life and renounce his many vices, definitely belongs to a Catholic world.

MOTIFS

As always, Shakespeare is keenly aware of the passage of time, aging, and death. When we first see Hal and Falstaff, they are bantering about what time of day it is. Falstaff is an old man, as we are often reminded (for example, when Hal teases him as "an old fat man" in the long tavern scene), but when he leads the robbery of the travelers he pretends otherwise, crying out (in the dark): "They hate us youth!" and "Young men must live."

Hotspur, on the other hand, has a kind of contempt for time itself, since, to him, it is nothing in comparison with honor. As he tells his own fellow rebels:

> O GENTLEMEN, THE TIME OF LIFE IS SHORT.
> TO SPEND THAT SHORTNESS BASELY WERE TOO LONG,
> IF LIFE DID RIDE UPON A DIAL'S POINT,
> STILL ENDING AT THE ARRIVAL OF AN HOUR.

Dying, after Hal has slain him, Hotspur will tell his vanquisher that "thou hast robbed me of my youth," but that he can better endure death than the loss of his "proud titles;" yet life, after all, must end eventually, and life is merely "time's fool." This is far from Falstaff's creed—"Give me life"—which puts survival above everything else and accepts honor only as something that may come "unlooked for."

Falstaff is well aware that this old world is a sinful one, and that he is part of it. "Dost thou hear, Hal?" (Even in those four simple syllables, his voice is unmistakable.)

> THOU KNOWEST IN THE STATE OF INNOCENCY ADAM
> FELL, AND WHAT SHOULD POOR JACK FALSTAFF DO IN
> THE DAYS OF VILLAINY? THOU SEEST I HAVE MORE FLESH
> THAN ANOTHER MAN AND THEREFORE MORE FRAILTY.

The practical Hal, as usual, falls between these extremes. He wants to make the best use of time, neither giving his life eagerly for honor, like Hotspur, nor making his physical survival an end in itself, as Falstaff does. He is willing to risk death in battle for the sake of achieving a great purpose, just as he is ready to betray friendships for the same purpose: namely, appearing worthy of royalty, the kingship he is to inherit from his father. He expresses his philosophy as common sense:

> IF ALL THE YEAR WERE PLAYING HOLIDAYS,
> TO SPORT WOULD BE AS TEDIOUS AS TO WORK.

Borrowing from Saint Paul's epistle to the Ephesians, he speaks of "redeeming time when men think least I will."

Another motif of the play is counterfeiting. Falstaff feigns death in battle (explaining later that "'twas time to counterfeit," or Douglas would have slain him in combat), then plays with the word as he stabs Hotspur's lifeless body in case "he should counterfeit too, and rise," still alive. "I am not a double man," he adds, when Hal is surprised to see him alive and well after the battle.

But the field is full of double men, such as the several decoys disguised, like Sir Walter Blunt, as the king. When Douglas encounters the real King Henry, he naturally wonders whether this is yet one more decoy: "I fear thou art another counterfeit." And, in a way, he may be right: From the rebels' point of view Henry is indeed a counterfeit king, a mere impersonator of royalty who can never be a legitimate ruler.

Hal, too, has been a double man all through the story, being one thing while pretending to be another and using others as his "foils" so that he can exploit the contrast between them and himself to his own advantage. He makes both Hotspur and Falstaff serve him this way. In the words of one commentator, Claire McEachern, Hal knows "how to manipulate signs and symbols and stories, to be master of all, but believe in none, or only to the outwardly convincing extent that is required to compel the belief of others."

Hal, a prodigal son, promises his distressed father that he will change. Falstaff also keeps saying he will reform, but this is a running joke, not a serious pledge. Hal really means it, though, and he is as good as his word, for it is something he has vowed to himself before he gave assurances to his father. As McEachern puts it, he is "a master of rhetorical appearances" who will prove to be "a consummately theatrical ruler" when he takes the throne as King Henry V. Yet these skills also imply that there is a good deal of hypocrisy in his makeup.

SYMBOLS

In the literature of Shakespeare's day, heavenly bodies—the sun, the moon, the planets, and the stars—can all stand for royalty. In his first soliloquy, Hal explicitly likens himself to the sun, currently dimmed by mists (meaning the tavern companions who now seem to disgrace him), but later to emerge in full glory and awe the world.

He and Falstaff also make complex and sophisticated jokes and puns about Phoebus, the sun, and Diana, the moon, as when Falstaff, referring to their nocturnal adventures as robbers, tells Hal:

> WHEN THOU ART KING, LET NOT US THAT ARE SQUIRES OF THE NIGHT'S BODY BE CALLED THIEVES OF THE DAY'S BEAUTY. LET US BE DIANA'S FORESTERS, GENTLEMEN OF THE SHADE, MINIONS OF THE MOON; AND LET MEN SAY WE BE MEN OF GOOD GOVERNMENT, BEING GOVERNED, AS THE SEA IS, BY OUR NOBLE AND CHASTE MISTRESS THE MOON, UNDER WHOSE COUNTENANCE WE STEAL.

Such rich witticisms, impressive as they may be to scholars, are extremely hard to paraphrase and, for the student, perhaps not worth the effort of detailed explanation. Footnotes requiring close concentration are rarely very funny. Once again we repeat that Shakespeare's language was never meant to be easy to take in; he meant it to be spoken rapidly. If much of it sounds archaic now, that is only part of its difficulty.

LANGUAGE

Shakespeare is the greatest master of the English language, but in *Henry IV*, much of the language is Elizabethan slang that is so outdated we can no longer understand it without footnotes. We must not let that slow us down. It is a mistake to try to understand every single word on the first reading.

The dialogue should move fast, as in a modern TV sitcom. A joke that has to be explained loses most of its fun, of course, so it is best to capture the rapid pace before we try to understand each line. Once again, hearing or watching a professional performance is a good way to start. Shakespeare did not write this play for scholars in their studies, but for rowdy theater audiences who had paid for an afternoon of fun.

The play is serious, but Falstaff is one of the world's greatest comic characters. And the rebel leader Hotspur is also very witty as he teases his wife, ridicules Glendower, and defies King Henry. *Henry IV* displays Shakespeare's comic gifts at their ripest, along with his genius for language. Once we get into the full swing of that language, especially in the scene of the Gad's Hill robbery and the famous tavern scene, we are in for inexpressible delight.

It is simply astounding that the creator of the hilarious Falstaff should also have written the most heart-wrenching tragedies of all time. How could one author achieve so much in one language? Shakespeare makes us realize how lucky we are to speak English. What he does could not have been done in any other language—even tongues as beautiful as Spanish and Italian. Once you regard reading Shakespeare as a privilege rather than a task, you are in for a lifetime of enjoyment. Shakespeare's versatility with language is vividly illustrated by the contrast between the philosophies of Hotspur and Falstaff regarding honor. For Hotspur, who aspires to heroism, honor is everything; he speaks of it in thrilling poetry and images of brave exploits:

[T]he blood more stirs
To rouse a lion than to start a hare.

He adds:

By heaven, methinks it were an easy leap

To pluck bright honor from the pale-faced moon,

Or dive into the bottom of the deep,

Where fathom line could never touch the ground

And pluck up drowned honor by the locks,

So he that doth redeem her thence might wear

Without corrival all her dignities. (Act I, Scene 3)

For the decidedly unheroic Falstaff, on the other hand, honor is a mere vanity, "a word," nothing but "air," something to put on coffins. In his only reflective soliloquy, he answers his own questions:

HONOR PRICKS ME ON. YEA, BUT HOW IF HONOR PRICK ME OFF WHEN I COME ON? HOW THEN? CAN HONOR SET TO A LEG? NO. OR AN ARM? NO. OR TAKE AWAY THE GRIEF OF WOUND? NO. HONOR HATH NO SKILL IN SURGERY, THEN? NO. WHAT IS HONOR? A WORD. WHAT IS IN THAT WORD "HONOR"? WHAT IS THAT "HONOR"? AIR. A TRIM RECKONING! WHO HATH IT? HE THAT DIED O' WEDNESDAY. DOTH HE FEEL IT? NO. DOTH HE HEAR IT? NO. 'TIS INSENSIBLE, THEN? YEA, TO THE DEAD. BUT WILL IT NOT LIVE WITH THE LIVING? NO. WHY? DETRACTION WILL NOT SUFFER IT. THEREFORE I'LL NONE OF IT. HONOR IS A MERE SCUTCHEON. AND SO ENDS MY CATECHISM. (ACT V, SCENE 1)

Unlike Hotspur, Falstaff speaks in earthy prose and short sentences, with his own humorous cynicism. "He that died o' Wednesday" is welcome to his useless honor, as far as Falstaff is concerned; the obese knight wants none of it. His observations that honor can neither set a broken limb nor heal a wound would never even occur to the idealistic Hotspur, who never expresses any fear of danger, pain, or death. Even Hotspur's verbs are active: He speaks of rousing a lion, leaping to the moon, diving to the bottom of the sea, plucking honor. Falstaff's imagination is passive; he is afraid of suffering. His question-and-answer "catechism" is a philosophy of cowardice. In his mind, courage is sheer folly. The two men are opposites in every respect, right down to the length and structure of their sentences. Together they provide one of the best examples of Shakespeare's genius for characterization.

INTERPRETING THE PLAY

Shakespeare seldom wrote a more colorful play, or one more packed with remarkable characters and settings, than *Henry IV*. It transports us from solemn councils in royal chambers to deserted highways after midnight and to crowded taverns where it always seems to be a noisy and bustling happy hour. Here indeed is the full flavor of humanity, the Bard's "infinite variety," the high tide of his creative genius. One of his best expositors says that "nothing he wrote is more crowded with life or happier in its imitation of human talk."

Although the entire *Henry IV* cycle is set around the year 1400, more than a century and a half before Shakespeare lived, it is full of the busy atmosphere of Elizabethan England. In it we seem to be hearing the vivid colloquial speech of its ordinary folk: servants, soldiers, tapsters, ostlers, travelers, whores, petty criminals, and the like.

Its happy anarchy provides a perfect setting for the indomitable Falstaff. Can we even imagine him anywhere else? And we seem to be there with him, sharing all the fun of the moment. What on earth will he do or say next? We know only that he will delight us with some sparkling sally of wit we would never have thought of ourselves. Just as Hal seems born to rule England, Falstaff was born to dominate the rowdy taverns of Eastcheap with unchallenged sovereignty.

FALSTAFF (FRED SULLIVAN, JR.)
HOLDS COURT AT THE TAVERN IN
THE 2004 TRINITY REPERTORY
COMPANY PRODUCTION.

The lowly denizens of the taverns, Falstaff's subjects, are also the people Hal is destined to rule, and he immerses himself in their element as if to learn their language and customs, like a foreign visitor, from his own experience. He does it superbly.

We ourselves also learn a great deal about that world. Mistress Quickly and her tavern associates, like the pirates and gravediggers in *Hamlet* or Bottom and his fellow tradesmen in *A Midsummer Night's Dream*, give us the living accents of London's common speech, as well as the manners of the time.

Henry IV is a highly iconoclastic play. It must have shocked its original audiences, who were used to the high-flown views of honor and glory voiced by both the king's partisans and the rebels. Falstaff's frank avowals of cowardice could only have seemed revolutionary, subversive of all received ideas, and therefore, like so much naughty and impious humor, extremely funny. He speaks for the ordinary man, eternally concerned for his own safety rather than for any noble cause or principle. Who will win the civil war that the chief characters are obsessed with is simply not his concern. In modern language, the fat knight is "politically incorrect." He is really many years too old to be on a battlefield in the first place, he has nothing at stake, and his cynicism keeps his head clear as he laughs at the illusions of others.

Another way to put it is that Falstaff is a very modern man, detached from old medieval loyalties and clichés. He refuses to be taken in by what

I'LL PURGE, AND LEAVE SACK, AND LIVE CLEANLY.

George Orwell would later call the "smelly little orthodoxies" of politics. He knows that partisans can make a glib case for any cause; instead of taking any of them seriously and arguing with them, he just rejects and mocks them all with an equal and impartial glee as he looks out for himself. His credo is elemental: "Give me life."

The story is continued, of course, in the second part of *Henry IV*, in which the rebellion is finally crushed, Henry IV dies, Hal becomes King Henry V, and Falstaff and his friends carry on with their mischievous doings until the new king, in a surprising reversal, cracks down on them.

Interest in this sequel has always centered on the banishment of Falstaff in the last scene. It is worth describing here in some detail.

Throughout the play, Sir John Falstaff has been his old self, as vivid, insolently witty, and inexhaustibly funny as ever (he never ceases to think of new jokes). But he has also been getting more and more presumptuous, defying the law (and the Lord Chief Justice, in particular) and thinking he will be able to get away with anything once his friend Hal becomes king. He has no sense of the limits that constrain all men, and his moral recklessness is part of what makes him so amusing.

At this point Falstaff's self-assurance knows no bounds. He is so confident that his fortunes will rise when Hal assumes the throne that he borrows a large sum of money from his old acquaintance Justice Shallow, thinking he will soon be able to repay it easily.

In fact, when the news of the old king's death reaches him, Falstaff's reaction is unmitigated triumph. Full of high expectation, he echoes the Bible one last time (failing to hear the blasphemy in his own words) as he promises his cronies high positions in the new order and invites them to come with him to greet the new King Henry V: "Let us take any man's horses. The laws of England are at my commandment. Blessed are they that have been my friends, and woe to my Lord Chief Justice!"

But he is in for a surprise—indeed, a severe shock. He addresses his old friend with public intimacy as "King Hal" and "thee," failing to realize that everything has now changed between them.

The king is enraged by Falstaff's endearments. He orders the Lord Chief Justice to "speak to that vain man." But when the Lord Chief Justice questions his sanity, Falstaff only gets worse, and the king himself must say something. He does, and he addresses the fat knight in scorching and sanctimonious terms:

> I KNOW THEE NOT, OLD MAN. FALL TO THY PRAYERS.
> HOW ILL WHITE HAIRS BECOME A FOOL AND JESTER.
> I HAVE LONG DREAMT OF SUCH A KIND OF MAN,
> SO SURFEIT-SWELLED, SO OLD, AND SO PROFANE;
> BUT BEING AWAKED, I DO DESPISE MY DREAM.
> MAKE LESS THY BODY HENCE, AND MORE THY GRACE;
> LEAVE GORMANDIZING; KNOW THE GRAVE DOTH GAPE
> FOR THEE THRICE WIDER THAN FOR OTHER MEN.
> REPLY NOT TO ME WITH A FOOL-BORN JEST;
> PRESUME NOT THAT I AM THE THING I WAS,
> FOR GOD DOTH KNOW SO SHALL THE WORLD PERCEIVE
> THAT I HAVE TURNED AWAY MY FORMER SELF.

Hal, now King Henry V, also orders Falstaff not to approach within ten miles of him. Then he brusquely departs with the Lord Chief Justice and his train of officers.

Devastated, Falstaff turns to Justice Shallow and says weakly, "Master Shallow, I owe you a thousand pound." When Shallow wants the money at once, Falstaff tries to stave him off and adds one last (and futile) bluff: "That can hardly be, Master Shallow. Do not you grieve at this. I shall be sent for in private to him. Look you, he must seem thus to the world. Fear not for your advancements. I will be the man yet that shall make you great."

But Shallow is not fooled, and he ridicules this empty boast. Even he can see that Falstaff is finished. The Lord Chief Justice returns with the officers, whom he orders to arrest Falstaff and all his followers and take them to the Fleet, London's chief prison.

The epilogue promises the audience another play showing King Henry in France, wooing the Princess Katharine and followed by Falstaff. But Falstaff never appears in *Henry V*. Instead, he dies. As he lies ill, Mistress Quickly says, "The king has killed his heart," and she later gives his old friends a pathetic account of his last moments of life. He kept crying out, "God, God, God," and talking of "green fields" (obviously trying to recite Psalm 23) as she did her best to comfort him. The poor woman kept covering his feet as he asked, but as she felt them, and then his knees, and then the rest of him, he was "as cold as any stone."

The confusedly affectionate reminiscences of these simple friends, appropriately comical, make for one of Shakespeare's most touching death scenes.

Falstaff seems to bear out Samuel Johnson's contention that Shakespeare's natural genius was even greater for comedy than for tragedy. In his 1765 edition of Shakespeare's plays, the usually restrained Johnson, himself a great humorist, nearly abandons self-control when he comments on the Bard's supreme comedian: "*Falstaff* unimitated, unimitable *Falstaff*, how shall I describe thee? Thou compound of sense and vice; of sense which may be admired, but not esteemed, of vice which may be despised, but hardly detested."

I CAN CALL SPIRITS FROM THE VASTY DEEP.

"BUT WILL THEY COME WHEN YOU DO CALL FOR THEM?"

A. C. Bradley's essay "The Rejection of Falstaff" in his *Oxford Lectures on Poetry* (1909) has rarely been surpassed as an analysis of the joyful power of the fat knight over our imaginations. He identifies that power as "the bliss of freedom gained in humor."

The studies of Harold Goddard (*The Meaning of Shakespeare*, 1951) and Mark Van Doren (*Shakespeare*, 1939) never fail to illuminate, and Van Doren is particularly perceptive and eloquent in his insights on Falstaff, which are as delightedly appreciative as his praise of Hamlet.

But others have taken a sterner view of the knight. John Dover Wilson's 1943 study *The Fortunes of Falstaff* rejected Bradley's Romantic approach in favor of a more moralistic judgment: the Elizabethans, he argued, would have approved of Hal's final repudiation of Falstaff as something that had to be done.

Chronology

1564   William Shakespeare is born on April 23 in Stratford-upon-Avon, England

1578–1582   Span of Shakespeare's "Lost Years," covering the time between leaving school and marrying Anne Hathaway of Stratford

1582   At age eighteen Shakespeare marries Anne Hathaway, age twenty-six, on November 28

1583   Susanna Shakespeare, William and Anne's first child, is born in May, six months after the wedding

1584   Birth of twins Hamnet and Judith Shakespeare

1585–1592   Shakespeare leaves his family in Stratford to become an actor and playwright in a London theater company

1587   Public beheading of Mary Queen of Scots

1593–94   The Bubonic (Black) Plague closes theaters in London

1594–96   As a leading playwright, Shakespeare creates some of his most popular work, including *A Midsummer Night's Dream* and *Romeo and Juliet*

1596   Hamnet Shakespeare dies in August at age eleven, possibly of plague

1596–97	*The Merchant of Venice* and *Henry IV, Part One* most likely are written
1599	The Globe Theater opens
1600	*Julius Caesar* is first performed at the Globe
1600–01	*Hamlet* is believed to have been written
1601–02	*Twelfth Night* is probably composed
1603	Queen Elizabeth dies; Scottish king James VI succeeds her and becomes England's James I
1604	Shakespeare pens *Othello*
1605	*Macbeth* is composed
1608–1610	London's theaters are forced to close when the plague returns and kills an estimated 33,000 people
1611	*The Tempest* is written
1613	The Globe Theater is destroyed by fire
1614	Reopening of the Globe
1616	Shakespeare dies on April 23
1623	Anne Hathaway, Shakespeare's widow, dies; a collection of Shakespeare's plays, known as the First Folio, is published

Source Notes

p. 75, par. 2, Goddard, Harold. The *Meaning of Shakespeare*. (Chicago: University of Chicago Press, 1951).

p. 78, par. 1, Sister Miriam Joseph. *Shakespeare's Use of the Arts of Language*. (Philadelphia: Paul Dry Books, 2005). This classic 1947 work is back in print and remains an invaluable guide for students of rhetoric as well as of Shakespeare.

p. 97, par. 1, Bradley, A.C. *Oxford Lectures on Poetry*. (London: Macmillan, 1909). Contains the famous essay "The Rejection of Falstaff."

p. 97, par. 2, Van Doren, Mark. *Shakespeare*. Garden City, NY: Doubleday, 1939.

p. 97, par. 3, Wilson, John Dover. *The Fortunes of Falstaff*. (Cambridge: Cambridge University Press, 1979). A stimulating study of Shakespeare's greatest comic character.

A Shakespeare Glossary

The student should not try to memorize these, but only refer to them as needed. We can never stress enough that the best way to learn Shakespeare's language is simply to *hear* it—to hear it spoken well by good actors. After all, small children master every language on earth through their ears, without studying dictionaries, and we should master Shakespeare, as much as possible, the same way.

addition —a name or title (knight, duke, duchess, king, etc.)
admire —to marvel
affect —to like or love; to be attracted to
an —if ("An I tell you that, I'll be hanged.")
approve —to prove or confirm
attend —to pay attention
belike —probably
beseech —to beg or request
betimes —soon; early
bondman —a slave
bootless —futile; useless; in vain
broil —a battle
charge —expense; responsibility; to command or accuse
clepe, clept —to name; named
common —of the common people; below the nobility
conceit —imagination
condition —social rank; quality
countenance —face; appearance; favor
cousin —a relative
cry you mercy —beg your pardon
curious — careful; attentive to detail
dear —expensive
discourse —to converse; conversation
discover —to reveal or uncover
dispatch —to speed or hurry; to send; to kill
doubt —to suspect

entreat —to beg or appeal

envy —to hate or resent; hatred; resentment

ere —before

ever, e'er —always

eyne —eyes

fain —gladly

fare —to eat; to prosper

favor —face, privilege

fellow —a peer or equal

filial —of a child toward its parent

fine —an end; in fine = in sum

fond —foolish

fool —a darling

genius —a good or evil spirit

gentle —well-bred; not common

gentleman —one whose labor was done by servants (Note: to call someone a *gentleman* was not a mere compliment on his manners; it meant that he was above the common people.)

gentles —people of quality

get —to beget (a child)

go to —"go on"; "come off it"

go we —let us go

haply —perhaps

happily —by chance; fortunately

hard by —nearby

heavy —sad or serious

husbandry —thrift; economy

instant —immediate

kind — one's nature; species

knave — a villain; a poor man

lady — a woman of high social rank (Note: *lady* was not a synonym for *woman* or *polite woman*; it was not a compliment, but, like *gentleman*, simply a word referring to one's actual legal status in society.)

leave — permission; "take my leave" = depart (with permission)

lief, lieve —"I had as lief" = I would just as soon; I would rather

like —to please; "it likes me not" = it is disagreeable to me

livery —the uniform of a nobleman's servants; emblem
mark —notice; pay attention
morrow —morning
needs —necessarily
nice —too fussy or fastidious
owe —to own
passing —very
peculiar —individual; exclusive
privy —private; secret
proper —handsome; one's very own ("his proper son")
protest —to insist or declare
quite —completely
require —request
several —different, various;
severally —separately
sirrah —a term used to address social inferiors
sooth —truth
state —condition; social rank
still —always; persistently
success —result(s)
surfeit —fullness
touching —concerning; about; as for
translate —to transform
unfold —to disclose
villain —a low or evil person; originally, a peasant
voice —a vote; consent; approval
vouchsafe —to confide or grant
vulgar —common
want —to lack
weeds —clothing
what ho —"hello, there!"
wherefore —why
wit —intelligence; sanity
withal —moreover; nevertheless
without —outside
would —wish

Suggested Essay Topics

1. Discuss Shakespeare's various treatments of power and its usurpation in *Henry IV*, *Hamlet*, *Julius Caesar*, and *Macbeth*.

2. Compare two of Shakespeare's most famous characters, Falstaff and Hamlet. Why do they continue to have such power over our imaginations?

3. Is Prince Hal justified in misleading his companions before he becomes king of England?

4. Henry IV is king of England. But is he a *legitimate* king? That is, do the people of England owe him their loyalty and obedience, as he assumes? This old question may never be settled, but give the arguments on both sides.

Testing Your Memory

1. How did Henry IV become king? a) by hereditary succession; b) by seizing the throne from the lawful king; c) by invasion; d) by election.
2. At the beginning of the play, the king hopes to travel with an army to a) Wales; b) the Holy Land; c) Scotland; d) France.
3. Falstaff is a) a knight; b) a duke; c) an earl; d) a court jester.
4. How does Prince Hal plan to treat Falstaff and his friends when he becomes king? a) He will promote them to high positions; b) He will reward their services to him; c) He will disown them; d) He will expose their crimes.
5. Who do the rebels want to be king? a) Richard II; b) Edmund Mortimer; c) Hotspur; d) Prince Hal.
6. Who does Hotspur call a "vile politician"? a) King Henry; b) Prince Hal; c) Falstaff; d) Owen Glendower.
7. While robbing the travelers, Falstaff pretends to be a) thin; b) drunk; c) needy; d) young.
8. Sack, Falstaff's favorite drink, is a) a dark ale; b) whiskey; c) gin; d) a Spanish sherry.
9. How many robbers took the money from Falstaff and his crew? a) fourteen; b) fifty; c) two; d) a hundred or so.
10. How does Falstaff mistreat Mistress Quickly? a) He cheats her out of money; b) He promises to marry her; c) He steals her horse; d) He slanders her to her neighbors.
11. Which character boasts of possessing supernatural powers? a) King Henry; b) Falstaff; c) Glendower; d) Hotspur.
12. Whom does King Henry accuse his son of resembling too much? a) King Richard II; b) Falstaff; c) Hotspur; d) his mother.

13. Who seems to be the one man King Henry fears most? a) Glendower; b) Hotspur; c) the Archbishop of York; d) Mortimer.

14. How does Falstaff abuse his command of the soldiers under his authority? a) He is too strict; b) He plays favorites; c) He allows them to bribe their way out of service; d) He exposes them to unnecessary dangers.

15. Hal singles out one man for his unexpected courage in battle. Who is he? a) Sir Walter Blunt; b) Sir John Falstaff; c) Sir Richard Vernon; d) Prince John of Lancaster.

16. Falstaff's "pistol" turns out to be a) a dull sword; b) a bottle of sack; c) a dagger of lath; d) a piece of wood carved to look like a small gun.

17. Who is killed while disguised as the king? a) the Earl of Worcester; b) Owen Glendower; c) Sir Walter Blunt; d) the Duke of Hereford.

18. How does Falstaff try to achieve military glory? a) He captures several important prisoners; b) He pretends to have killed Hotspur; c) He leads a charge against the rebels; d) He tries to sacrifice his own life to save Hal.

19. Who decides to deceive the rebels about the king's peace offering? a) Hotspur; b) the Earl of Worcester; c) Sir Walter Blunt; d) Ned Poins.

20. Who is the valiant rebel whose life Prince Hal spares? a) the Earl of Worcester; b) the Earl of Douglas; c) Glendower; d) Mortimer.

Answer Key

12. a; 13. d; 14. d; 15. d; 16. b; 17. c; 18. b; 19. b; 20. b

1. b; 2. b; 3. a; 4. c; 5. b; 6. a; 7. d; 8. d; 9. c; 10. a; 11. c;

Further Information

BOOKS

The Annotated Shakespeare. *Henry IV, Part 1*. New Haven, CT: Yale University Press, 2006.

Oxford School Shakespeare. *Henry IV, Part 1*. New York: Oxford University Press, 2008. An edition especially designed for students with on-page notes and clear background information.

WEBSITES

http://absoluteshakespeare.com
  Summaries of the Bard's plays, poems, sonnets, and famous quotes

http://www.williamshakespeare.info/site-map.htm
  Shakespeare biography and history of the plague in Europe

FILMS

Despite its popularity on the stage, *Henry IV* has rarely been put on film. Yet one remarkable version does exist, the great Orson Welles's 1965 treatment, *Chimes at Midnight*, which combines both parts, along with a few passages from *Richard II*. Welles himself directed it brilliantly and starred as the corpulent Falstaff, making full use of his huge girth, booming voice, and great wit. The cast also included such Shakespearean luminaries as Sir John Gielgud in the role of King Henry IV and Margaret Rutherford as Mistress Quickly.

The BBC Shakespeare Histories DVD set includes five plays (*Henry IV* Parts 1 and 2, *Henry V, Richard II*, and *Richard III*) starring some of Britain's finest actors: Jon Finch as King Henry, Anthony Quayle as Falstaff, Tim Pigott-Smith as Hotspur, and David Gwillim as Prince Hal. English subtitles help viewers follow the dialogue.

AUDIO

Several fine recordings of *Henry IV*, Part 1, exist, one of the most notable being the Caedmon version, directed by Howard Sackler and featuring Sir Anthony Quayle as Falstaff and Sir Michael Redgrave as Hotspur.

The Arkangel Complete Shakespeare group produced a fine recording in 2005, featuring Julian Glover as King Henry, Jamie Glover as Prince Hal, and Richard Griffiths as Falstaff.

Bibliography

General Commentary

Bate, Jonathan, and Eric Rasmussen, eds. *William Shakespeare Complete Works (Modern Library)*. New York: Random House, 2007.

Bloom, Harold. *Shakespeare: The Invention of the Human*. New York: Riverhead Books, 1998.

Garber, Marjorie. *Shakespeare After All*. New York: Pantheon, 2004.

Goddard, Harold C. *The Meaning of Shakespeare*. Chicago: University of Chicago Press, 1951.

Traversi, D. L. *An Approach to Shakespeare*. Palo Alto, CA: Stanford University Press, 1957.

Van Doren, Mark. *Shakespeare*. Garden City, NY: Doubleday, 1939.

Biography

Burgess, Anthony. *Shakespeare*. New York: Alfred A. Knopf, 1970.

Chute, Marchette. *Shakespeare of London*. New York: Dutton, 1949.

Greenblatt, Stephen. *Will in the World: How Shakespeare Became Shakespeare*. New York: W. W. Norton & Company, 2004.

Honan, Park. *Shakespeare: A Life*. New York: Oxford University Press, 1998.

Schoenbaum, Samuel. *William Shakespeare: A Documentary Life*. New York: Oxford University Press, 1975.

———. *William Shakespeare: Records and Images*. New York: Oxford University Press, 1981.

Index

Page numbers in **boldface** are illustrations.

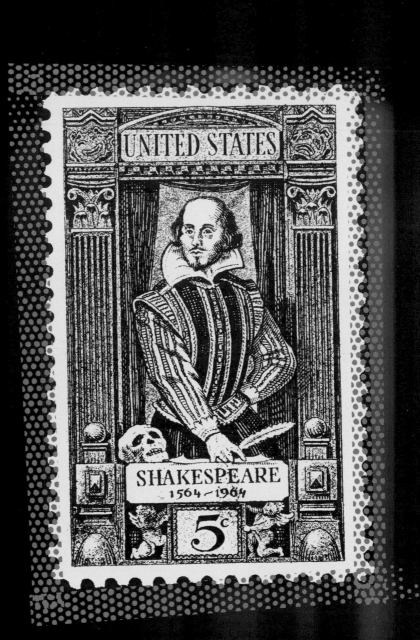

About the Author

Joseph Sobran is the author of several books, including *Alias Shakespeare* (1997). He lives in northern Virginia.